BEASTLY JOURNEYS

JOURNEYS

UNUSUAL TALES OF
TRAVEL WITH ANIMALS

Compiled and edited by
Hilary Bradt and Jennifer Barclay

First published June 2018
Bradt Travel Guides Ltd
IDC House, The Vale, Chalfont St Peter, Bucks SL9 9RZ, England
www.bradtguides.com

Print edition published in the USA by The Globe Pequot Press Inc,
PO Box 480, Guilford, Connecticut 06437-0480

Text copyright © 2018 Bradt Travel Guides
Introduction by Hilary Bradt
Edited by Jennifer Barclay and Hilary Bradt
Copy-edited by Ian Smith
Proofread by Adrian Dixon
Cover design: illustration and concept by Neil Gower
Typesetting by Ian Spick
Digital conversion by www.dataworks.co.in
Production managed by Sue Cooper and Jellyfish Print Solutions
Printed in the UK

ISBN: 978 1 78477 081 5 (print)
e-ISBN: 978 1 78477 545 2 (e-pub)
e-ISBN: 978 1 78477 296 3 (mobi)

British Library Cataloguing in Publication Data
A catalogue record for this book is available from the British Library

Many thanks to the following: Hodder and Stoughton for permission to use an excerpt
from *Zoo Quests: The Adventures of a Young Naturalist*, © David Attenborough (1959)
(published by arrangement with the Lutterworth Press); Curtis Brown Group Ltd, London,
on behalf of the Estate of Gerald Durrell for permission to use an excerpt from *The
Whispering Land*, © Gerald Durrell (1964); Bloomsbury Publishing USA and the Headline
Publishing Group for permission to use an excerpt from *Zarafa: A Giraffe's True Story, from
Deep in Africa to the Heart of Paris*, © Michael Allin (1999); Max Hastings on behalf of
the Estate of Michael Joseph for permission to use an excerpt from *Charles: The Story of a
Friendship*, © Michael Joseph (1943); Max Press for permission to adapt an excerpt from
The Sky is on Fire, © Magsie Hamilton Little (2017); Eland Books for permission to use an
excerpt from *Travels on my Elephant*, © Mark Shand (1992); and Bloomsbury Publishing
Plc. for permission to use an excerpt from *Tracks*, © Robyn Davidson (1980).

Table of Contents

Introduction

Hilary Bradt

My earliest recollection of travelling with animals was when I was around six years old. Admittedly I'd only carried the snails from the bus stop to my primary school in their sealed-in hibernation state (it was winter). But I was summoned from the classroom by the headmistress.

'Come with me, Hilary,' she boomed, and led me to the cloakroom. There was my navy-blue regulation woollen coat, hanging with those of the other little girls, and all were covered in a network of slimy trails ending in happily exploring snails. The trails radiated out from my coat pocket. The warmth of the cloakroom had felt like the call of spring, and the snails were hungry.

My lifelong love of invertebrates has led to challenges, such as the incident of the cruise ship and the Madagascan hissing cockroach, a species I'm particularly fond of, having kept them as pets. I was lecturing on an expedition ship and thought it would be educational for the passengers to see that not all cockroaches are scuttling winged creatures; the ones in Madagascar live in holes in trees, and hiss engagingly if disturbed. But this one escaped in my cabin and I had no choice but to continue with the ship to the Comoros and hope I could capture it before the cleaning staff arrived in the morning. I imagined the entire ship being evacuated for health and safety reasons and losing its licence. Fortunately the cockroach was tempted into a trap I made with fruit secreted from the buffet.

A more successful import from Madagascar was Millicent the giant pill millipede who made it to England disguised as a piece of camera equipment. She lived for over a year in an aquarium, though I must admit she was probably the most boring pet I've ever kept. Much more interesting – at least in the response it elicited from my fellow bus passengers – was the Jackson's chameleon that I captured in a park in Nairobi. These little chameleons have three impressive horns at the end of their noses, and I had been looking for one ever since I arrived in east Africa. I popped the little fellow into the only container I had, a brown paper bag, so I could take him back to my hotel for the night to study and photograph. He had other ideas and used his horns to burst through the paper like a miniature circus act and glare around the bus with that down-at-the-mouth expression worn by all chameleons. The result was dramatic. The bus erupted into screams as men rushed for the door and the driver screeched to a stop. I'd forgotten the superstitious fear of chameleons shared by many Africans.

The big trip, however, was with an animal universally loved and valued: a pony. My travels with Peggy feature in this collection of stories, along with several others with pack or riding animals. Ever since large animals were domesticated for the purpose of carrying people and their luggage on long journeys, they have accompanied humans on their travels. It's only during the last century that this became a choice rather than a necessity, and the bond between animal and human was recognised as a key part of the journey. Two book extracts highlight the contrast between George Borrow, writing about his horse difficulties in Spain in 1835, and his modern counterpart in Peru, Dervla Murphy, and her love for her mule Juana.

It was the tale of a street dog which attached itself to a traveller to enjoy some food and affection, transforming the visitor's experience of the place where they met, that inspired us to begin collecting stories about animals as travel companions. With dogs and cats it is natural to form a bond, but we were surprised by the range of animals that connected with travellers in the stories we read, from a humble sparrow to a giraffe. We were looking not for stories of wildlife-spotting but a journey with an animal, and we hope the collection has something for everyone, from the moving tale of a race against time for an orphaned baby elephant to the farcical story of smuggling a very small tortoise through five international borders.

The animals in these stories are as varied as the journeys, large and small, domestic or wild, compliant or reluctant. All, in their way, made the human journey special and all remind us of the affection that we humans feel for animals.

THE
AMERICAS

From *Zoo Quest in Paraguay*

Sir David Attenborough

In 1954, a young David Attenborough was offered the opportunity to travel the world finding rare animals for London Zoo's collection, and to film the expeditions for the BBC.

When we had first arrived in Paraguay, I had confirmed that the only practical way of flying a cargo of animals from Asunción to London was through the United States. It was a long way round, there was the possibility that we might be delayed in making our connections and, as it was now December, we should be faced with the problem of finding heated accommodation for the collection during the time we should have to spend in New York. It was not an ideal route but we believed it to be the only one.

Then Sandy told us that by chance he had met the local representation of a European airline who had claimed that he could quite easily arrange for us to fly direct from Buenos Aires to Europe, thereby reducing the journey by many hours. This would be a far more satisfactory arrangement and we rushed round to the airline office to find out the details. Sandy's friend confirmed that this was indeed possible, for, he said, although there were no freighters crossing the Atlantic from Buenos Aires, many of his company's passenger planes were returning from South America three-quarters empty at this time of year and he was certain that he could get special permission for one of them to take us and our menagerie. All that he required was a list of the animals. With alacrity we produced a copy of the exhaustive catalogue we had produced for the customs authorities which listed the sex, size and age in years and months of every animal we possessed.

He read it through out loud, in a wondering tone of voice. When he came to the armadillos, his brow furrowed and he reached down a bulky manual of regulations. After studying the index for some considerable time, he looked up at us.

'What are those animals, please?'

'Armadillos. They are rather charming little creatures, actually, with hard protective shells.'

'Oh, tortoises.'

'No. Armadillos.'

'Maybe they are a kind of lobster.'

'No, they are not lobsters,' I said patiently. 'They are armadillos.'

'What is their name in Spanish?'

'Armadillo.'

'In Guarani?'

'Tatu.'

'And in English?'

'Strangely enough,' I said jocularly, 'armadillo.'

'Gentlemen,' he said, 'you must be mistaken. There must be some other name for them, because armadillo is not mentioned in the regulations and *all* animals are listed in here.'

'I am sorry,' I replied, 'but that is their name and they have no other.'

He shut up his book with a bang.

'Never mind,' he said gaily, 'I will call them something else. I am sure it will be all right.'

On the strength of his assurances, we cancelled the elaborate arrangements we had made to travel via New York.

Two days before we were due to leave Asunción, the airlines man reappeared at the house with a worried look on his face.

'I am very sorry,' he said, 'but my company cannot accept your cargo. Head office in Buenos Aires say that those animals that were not mentioned in the manual will smell too bad.'

'Nonsense,' I said indignantly, 'our armadillos do not smell at all. What did you say they were?'

'I just called them something which I was sure that no-one would have heard of before. I could not remember the name you said so I found one in my son's animal book.'

'What did you say they were?' I repeated.

'Skunks,' he replied.

Sir David Attenborough is a broadcaster and naturalist whose television career is now in its seventh decade. After studying natural sciences at Cambridge and a brief stint in publishing, he joined the BBC. Since the launch of his famous *Zoo Quest* series in 1954 he has surveyed almost every aspect of life on earth and brought it to the viewing public. His latest programme, *Planet Earth II*, was the most-watched nature documentary of all time.

The Llama that Couldn't

Gordon Thompson

The summer of my freshman year in college, I joined a two-man trail crew in the Frank Church – River of No Return Wilderness in Idaho, at a Forest Service guard station accessible only by Cessna, more than a hundred miles from the nearest paved road.

I shared a log cabin with Matt, another college kid, while Rolf and Margaret, the middle-aged ranger and his wife, occupied another. There was also a tack cabin, a food storage/laundry/bathing cabin, a woodshed and an outhouse, together forming an island of human order amidst 2.3 million acres of coniferous mountains where it snowed in July. Elk herds several hundred strong roiled the impossibly starry nights with their otherworldly trumpeting, as if mourning the thousands of acres that had burned three summers before, the fire rushing toward the guard station 'like a freight train', Rolf said, only to walk right by and leave it unscathed.

Packing for the four-day loops of trail clearing Matt and I went on was always a bit agonising, since we'd feel every extra ounce in our legs.

'Maybe we should just bring peanut butter this time, and skip the jam,' I said as Matt and I sorted gear in our cabin lit by propane lantern. 'It kills me to carry that glass jar.'

'Eh, who cares?' Matt said. 'Let the llamas carry it.'

'*Let the llamas do it*,' I repeated, tossing in another brick of cheese. 'That has a nice ring to it.'

While Matt and I were out on our last four-day loop, an outfitter had brought in two llamas for us to use as pack animals on future excursions. Rolf gave us a crash course in caring for them, and we looked forward to leaving our big backpacks behind. It sounded great. No longer would we have to hump forty-pound packs up and down long, steep, rugged trails in search of downed trees, slogging them off to untie the Pulaski and two-man crosscut saw we'd use to cut the deadfall out, and then slogging them back on to continue hiking. The llamas would carry everything, even some oats for themselves, and we could quickly grab the saw and Pulaski right off their backs.

True to form, they were gentle, quiet and agreeable. Henry, the white one, was taller than I was with his neck extended, and he didn't mind my rubbing it; sometimes he hummed when I petted him. Hector, black and white like a giant border collie, was smaller and a bit skittish, seeming to look to Henry for direction. We were warned that they might kick if we approached in their blind spots and they might spit if they felt threatened, but nothing seemed to provoke them, even when we cinched their saddles and loaded them up with fifty pounds of gear apiece. With big dark eyes, enormous lashes, delicate ears, protuberant lips and spindly, knock-kneed legs, they had an oddly feminine look, even though they were hung like horses.

On the second day of the loop, Henry started getting balky, stopping in the middle of the uphill trail and jerking his head back when I tried to coax him forward. I called his name, I tugged on his bridle, I rubbed his neck, I made clicking noises, but he wouldn't budge.

'Maybe he's hungry,' Matt said. 'I'll get some oats.'

By the time Matt retrieved a handful of oats, Henry had begun grazing, and he made no move to stop. Hector was grazing too – that's what herbivores do, I'd learned. How wonderful never to carry food, the main thing weighing Matt and me down; subsisting on whatever you could lean down and grab seemed great until I considered that most of my waking life would be spent chewing.

'Should we just let him graze awhile?' I said.

'Doesn't look like we have much choice,' Matt said. A champion cross-country runner, Matt didn't take kindly to standing still.

When Henry ran out of grass, he was ready to move again, but ten minutes later he stopped short once more.

This pattern repeated itself every ten or fifteen minutes for nearly two hours, until the trail finally flattened out. Rolf had told us that the best way to lead a llama was by looping the rope around your waist and walking normally; the llama would match whatever pace you set. For the last two hours I felt I was in a tractor-pull, the rope digging into my belly like an outgrown belt. We switched off repeatedly to make sure Henry didn't have a grudge against me, but he was just as stubborn with Matt.

Things went well for the next half-mile, which was mostly flat, but when we got to another uphill section, it wasn't long before Henry refused to move again – only this time, he sat down, his legs disappearing under him and a spear of grass sticking out from his split lip. His kinship to a camel – and a yogi – was never clearer.

'Do you think he's breathing kinda hard?' Matt said.

'Maybe,' I said, touching his neck. 'Hard to tell with all that fur.'

'I'm gonna walk ahead with Hector. Rolf said they're very social animals, so Henry'll probably follow if he thinks he's being left behind.'

'Worth a try.'

A few minutes later Matt returned with Hector.

'What's the matter?' I said.

'As soon as Hector gets out of sight of Henry, he refuses to continue.'

'Are you shitting me?'

'I guess he doesn't want to leave his friend.'

'You take Henry,' I said. 'Let me try going ahead with Hector.'

'Sure.'

It was uncanny. Hector would walk out of sight of Henry, but then, without so much as a backward glance, he reached an invisible line of distance and stopped dead, unwilling to continue for all the coaxing and tugging in the world. As I stood there trying to get him moving so Henry might get moving, it occurred to me that 'domestic animal' was an oxymoron. Each of these llamas was several times bigger than I was, and when push came to shove they served at their pleasure, not mine. In a world of machines, we forget that animals have free will, and must be tended, not driven.

'No dice, huh?' Matt said when I returned.

'If we keep on at this rate, we won't make camp before dark.'

'I'm about ready to try carrying the gear ourselves, but we can't, because we only have daypacks.'

It was humbling to admit we needed the llamas more than they needed us.

Henry wouldn't get up until he was good and ready, so we spent the rest of the day on 'llama time'. Margaret had shown us a clipping about llamas on the Pacific Crest Trail: 'Furry friends carry everything from chairs to cantaloupes,' it claimed, freeing hikers to stroll unencumbered through scenic wonderland. 'Llama time' was supposed to spell luxury and ease, but for us it had become frustration and rage.

We were stuck with Henry and Hector for three more days – saddling and unsaddling them, leading them to water, picketing them at night, dragging them along the trail, waiting while Henry staged sit-in after sit-in, all the while moving slower than if we'd been our own beasts of burden. Sometimes we got so frustrated we kicked at roots and winged rocks at trees. Once I was sitting down collecting pine cones to kill time, and without thinking I started throwing them at Henry.

'Dude!' Matt said.

Barely listening, I kept showering Henry with tiny brown bombs.

'*Dude!*' Matt yelled.

I stopped mid-throw.

'What are you doing?' Matt said.

I was dumbstruck.

'He's not gonna move. Just forget it.'

Henry had barely registered being hit, but I was suddenly ashamed, and dropped my remaining pine cones. I'd never picked a fight with a human; why was I attacking an animal? Always tiring quicker than Matt, I was anxious to keep up – but that wasn't Henry's fault. If anything, I should identify with him; all too often I'd been the weakling, the straggler.

'It's pretty funny if you think about it,' Matt said.

'Me?'

'You. Me. Henry. The whole picture of us dragging this sorry pair of llamas along, stopping every fifteen minutes…'

'I wasn't going to hurt him.'

'I know. And I'm not laughing at you, or the llamas. Henry must have a heart condition or something.'

'Maybe he's just lazy.'

'A l-lazy llama? Now that's a l-laugh!'

'A l-lazy llama no-one could l-love. L-look out for that.'

We kept upping the ante of silly alliteration until we could hardly breathe for laughing.

By the time we hiked back to the guard station it was clear there was something wrong with Henry beyond stubbornness.

'Some people just aren't cut out for work,' Rolf said, after we'd returned Henry and Hector to their little pasture. 'Some animals neither.'

I couldn't tell if Rolf was being ironic. He was an enigmatic man who turned every word over like a chess piece before uttering it, a sly grin forever folded into his tanned face. It was silly to assume all animals were the same, but on the other hand, hadn't llamas evolved over thousands of years precisely to *be* pack animals?

'I hate to pack 'em out again so soon,' Rolf continued, 'but they're no use to us if they can't walk.'

'What will they do with 'em?' Matt said.

'I'm sure somebody'll find a use for them. If worse comes to worst, they can always go to a petting zoo. For now they're government property, just like you and me…'

I remembered the green pick-ups and cargo vans gathering dust in the auction lot, the scrap heap of rusty Pulaskis and broken parachute packs in the huge smokejumpers' prep shed back in McCall. Would the llamas be discarded so easily? Angry as Henry had made me, I hated to think of him being sent away like an incorrigible schoolboy. Apart from a stray cat I'd rescued as a kid, he and Hector were the closest I'd come to having pets. They didn't belong in these mountains, but neither did I.

Matt and I spent the next week working on nearby trail renovations, sleeping in our cabin every night. Henry and Hector were nearly self-sufficient, but every afternoon I visited them, offering oats and neck rubs. Often Henry hummed while I petted him – whether longing for his homeland, apologising for failing as a pack animal, or acknowledging physical pleasure, I wasn't sure. It's one thing to make a twelve-pound housecat purr; it's quite another to make a four-hundred-pound llama hum. In those moments I felt closer to the wild than when the elk herds trumpeted, or I stood alone atop a windy peak, or looked up while hiking to see pine trees echoing to infinity in all directions, their canopy so thick it blotted out the sun.

The following week Matt and I went on another four-day loop, and when we got back the llamas were gone.

Having earned an MFA from the University of Florida, **Gordon Thompson** teaches at the Cranbrook Schools in metro Detroit. He has also built trails with the Forest Service, served as a Kiva Fellow, and worked, studied and travelled in more than fifty countries.

Running with Parrots

Katharine Lowrie

A small flock of austral parakeets scratched for seeds in the snow. Snowflakes gently settled on their feathers. Their plumage was an exquisite collection of leaf, emerald and olive greens, sea and sky blues, with a scarlet tail and belly patch, all fluffed up into a feather duvet. When most people picture parakeets, they're cackling through steaming forests, not grubbing about in the freezer of a Patagonian winter. It was as if they had misread their contracts and their internal routing systems had malfunctioned.

We ran on, with snow underfoot and parakeets filling the air, basking in the glorious contradictions.

My husband David and I had chosen to run the length of South America, a distance of 6,504 miles, because we wanted to inspire environmental action: to prove that with small steps we can tackle seemingly insurmountable challenges. It's not too late to protect the world's remaining unspoilt ecosystems, but time is running out. We were raising money for nature conservation and speaking to remote communities, people who had never been visited by their own kinsfolk – let alone a pair of gringos emerging barefoot from the forest, spattered in brick-red Amazon mud and pulling a bright-orange bamboo trailer.

We both adore running. It's what we do to relax, feel free, go wild and ignite ideas. Every vista holds something new: a peregrine free falling through the sky; a hare dashing over a hilltop. Thoughts flow and ebb through your mind, sometimes conscious, sometimes lurking beyond. They move in time with the rhythm of your footfall and the exhalation of your breath. It's as if your senses are freshly tuned, tingling and raw, as your feet feel the ground beneath you and the wind and rain pulls at your body.

But the crucial element is running wild, running with wildlife and wilderness. Running allows us to penetrate the moods of the land and its creatures. With only a couple of millimetres of 'barefoot' shoe soles separating us from the earth's heartbeat, often only our unshod skin, we move silently, stealthily, creeping up on wildlife, a whisper away from discovery, a step from the unknown and unexpected.

We hadn't expected to be accompanied by parrots of every shape, colour and size. Parrots watched over us from the toe of the continent, where we waded waist-deep through snow, through Argentina's oven in temperatures reaching forty-five degrees Celsius, to the Amazon rainforest and finally over the coastal mountains to the Caribbean Sea.

A shiver of fear flickered through my senses as we left Las Lajas, Argentina. Ahead lay a forbidding expanse of desert. We were following a road, but traffic was infrequent and passed at breakneck speed, and the expanse of nothingness felt all-pervading, stretching for mile upon windswept mile. Suddenly, screeching filled the air as an unexpected flock of birds bombed into view. They were back – our guardians, the parrots!

This time their plumage was more muted to suit the ochre-coloured territory they inhabited; olive, with grey breast and yellow belly, blotched scarlet. Their eyes seemed huge, with white halos and upward streaks, as if they had been at the eyeliner and painted their tummies with lipstick. These were burrowing parrots, a species I had read about, but never imagined we would actually run with. But how on earth could they live here in such a barren land?

Evidently they had eaten whatever it was they had found to feed upon, and now were streaming back to a colony of nests excavated in an unconsolidated limestone cliff by the side of the road – our road. Heads poked out of the Swiss-cheese rock, scrutinising us; some preened, others shrieked, all within their tight pair bonds.

During the next four days, over some eighty miles, we ran with burrowing parrots shooting across our path – our friends in this hostile land. We started to glean a clue as to what they were foraging upon, watching them carefully picking seeds from spiny shrubs and tiny herbs on the ground. Then, one day, as suddenly as they had appeared, they were gone. Silence fizzed in our ears. Perhaps we had run beyond their commuting range? Perhaps this zone was bereft of the food they sought? Whatever their reasons, we ran alone, with heavy hearts.

So our feet carried us ever northwards, often unshod (we would run a third of the distance barefoot), sensing the crenulations and warmth of the tarmac, seeking the cool of the white lines dashing the road, the two trailer wheels spinning behind one or the other of us, eyes and ears sieving the air. But it wasn't long before our faithful friends returned in the guise of beautiful purple-and-emerald scaly-headed parrots crashing out of trees as we passed, and a flock of mitred parakeets screaming through the valley below us, gravitating upon a grove of trees groaning with fruit.

In Bolivia, our daily parrot encounters soared and with them our mood. Well before dawn we would extract ourselves from a camp deep in the forest, fumbling with kit and stumbling in a sleep-deprived fog. Suddenly our senses would be electrified by parrots cartwheeling and cackling through the air in a flash of colours. Yellow-collared macaws, scaly-headed parrots, turquoise-fronted parrots and blue-crowned parakeets burst into our lives. Often they would be feeding in the treetops or commuting between their favourite roosting sites. But upon spying us, at least one or two individuals would break off from the flock, beelining for us and craning their necks to gain a better view, clearly intrigued as to what species we might be.

The heart-warming sound of blue-fronted parrots, or *habladores* (literally the 'chatty ones' in Spanish), tumbling through the morning sky and gurgling to one another and, it seemed, to us, filled our daily marathon with joy. We marvelled at their knowledge of the area and wondered how their internal compass led them so meticulously to their favourite trees, just in time for a fruiting bonanza. Unfortunately, their skill and intelligence and of course their fantastic talent for mimicry make them a much-desired pet. And so we witnessed, the length of South America, these garrulous characters transformed into highly distressed, flea-bitten captives imprisoned in metal cages or clinging on to a bar of steel, eking an existence from chewing on a piece of hard white bread.

There was one particular parrot we sought, a species so rare that its population teeters on the edge of extinction: the blue-throated macaw, or 'Barba Azul', 'Bluebeard', as it is known in Bolivia, the only country in the world where it can be found. It was the species we were raising money for through our charity Asociación Armonía. The reasons for the macaw's demise are similar to those that have endangered many other parrots; one is a toxic pet trade, the other dramatic habitat loss. Without a home, which for the blue-throated macaw includes motacú palm islands for nesting, roosting and foraging in, the birds cannot survive. Over the years their habitat has been relentlessly removed through overgrazing of the palm islands, and the burning and seeding of non-native, aggressive African grasses, to increase the pasture available for the enormous herds that provide cheap beef to countries around the world.

Asociación Armonía established where the main flocks of the macaw were, then worked with the estancia owners to ensure their land management considered the macaw's needs, erected nest boxes and initiated twenty-four-hour surveillance during the nesting season. The next step was to buy a reserve which they could manage specifically for the macaws.

So we took a couple of days off from running and set out on horseback with Jernan, the reserve warden, through a network of lagoons and grassland in the remote Barba Azul Reserve in search of this enigmatic macaw. Tall grasses and reeds swept the horses' bellies as we edged around the swamp. We were making for the distant palm islands, far beyond the research centre, where blue-throated macaws commute for feeding.

A volley of barks exploded from the vegetation in front of us. Enormous guinea pigs galloped for the water, detonating a wave of spray from under their hairy legs. They were capybaras, the largest rodents in the world, and they reminded me of a gaggle of overweight Edwardian bathing ladies. Shocked by our appearance, they disappeared under the water. But after a few minutes, faces began to pop up beside the lily pads and rushes, like little hairy hippos, curious about us – as curious as we were about them.

A large party of American wood storks were patrolling the shallows a little further on, like expectant undertakers with their 'arms' held behind their backs and long, downward-pointing, thinking 'noses'. Wetlands are always wildlife magnets and, even as we left the swamp, we looked up to see the sky full with skeins of storks gliding towards it from the surrounding grasslands. Then something crashed into the corner of our view. A cloud of macaws was streaking overhead.

We counted sixteen in total. They called to one another, piercing the air with their repetitive, hoarse shrieks. Could this be them: a party of one of the rarest birds on earth? We could see only their silhouettes at first, and neither of us could tell the difference between the more raucous call of the blue-and-yellow macaws and the slightly lighter call of the blue-throats. But Jernan knew. Our three sets of eyes met and he nodded, grinning. It *was* them. As if answering our wishes, the birds broke off to the south, flying directly over us. As they drew closer we watched their dark shapes transform into a dazzling display of gold and indigo. I wished I could burn their images on to my retinas for eternity.

Returning to the reality of running and life on the road was hard. But soon our parrot family found us, softening the blow. Blue-and-yellow macaws flapped at our side and one afternoon more than two hundred peach-fronted parakeets exploded from a thicket of trees near our camp. Somehow the countryside absorbed these colourful beauties into its soft pallet of hues, so that only movement or sound revealed their presence.

But it was in northern Brazil where our parrot friendship reached new levels. Orange-winged parrots, our daily running companions, were gurgling in the treetops as we trotted up a gravel track, through grassland with scattered trees and wooden bungalows. Suddenly something swooped at David's head: a gorgeous, vivid-green, yellow-crowned parrot. It looked down at us from a branch, chortling contentedly. We chatted back, watching it as we ran. Then something remarkable happened: it followed us.

As we ran it would fly forward over our heads and then dive-bomb David before flapping off to a perch. This continued for three or four miles, until I stopped to tie my shoelace. While I was leaning over, I felt a light weight on my back. The parrot had landed on me.

Gradually I stood up, and as I did so it walked up my back to my shoulder. For someone who loves wildlife, for someone who loves birds, this was incredible – one of the best moments of my life! We walked on, an unusual trio, me with an apparently contented parrot gently nibbling my ear (which, considering the parrot uses its formidable beak for cracking palm nuts, was very trustworthy, or just plain idiotic, on my part). I tried preening its back, but it squealed. That was clearly too forward a move at this delicate stage in our relationship. Then I slipped in a puddle, and it was gone, flapping high into a tree. We called for it as we ran on, but it didn't follow. David was sure we would see it again, but we never did.

Adapted from *Running South America with my Husband and other animals* by Katharine Lowrie.

Katharine Lowrie is an ecologist who has worked in nature conservation in the UK, Zambia, South Africa, New Zealand and the Caribbean. She currently works part-time for the RSPB and spends the rest of her time writing and outside with her two young children. For a signed and dedicated copy of the book. visit: www.5000mileproject.org/shop.

From *Eight Feet in the Andes*

Dervla Murphy

In 1978 Dervla Murphy and her nine-year-old daughter, Rachel, assisted by a mule named Juana, trekked thirteen hundred (or so) miles through the Andes from Cajamarca to Cuzco. Over much of their planned route there weren't even footpaths marked on any available map. Both travellers kept a daily diary on which Eight Feet in the Andes *is based.*

7th October

I'm trying to conceal my forebodings from Rachel but I'm worried. This morning poor Juana went very lame, suddenly. In such relentlessly rugged country no tent site appeared until 10.30 a.m. when we'd covered scarcely six miles because Juana could only hobble. As we know nothing about equine complaints we can't make a diagnosis; there's nothing visibly wrong. She has become so beloved that neither of us, I suspect, would have the will to continue with another animal. Maybe this sounds too sentimental but when the going gets rough her unflappability gives us invaluable moral support. Here is a perfect hospital site, an acre of soft springy turf on which Juana reclined all day in the warm sunshine with Rachel lying reading beside her. Towards sunset the temperature dropped melodramatically and then for a little time I sat on a rock, alone with the skyscape of pale delicate clouds interwoven with dark fearsome peaks. One more memorable moment...

8th October

Alas! my dream of Huari as a problem-solving *pueblo* has not come true. There is no *veterinario* and the alfalfa supply is poor. Behind the dosshouse Juana must share a corral with five pigs who, left to themselves, would gobble her supper within moments. So I've had to sit with her for two hours, reading by torchlight and aiming frequent kicks at porcine marauders.

Chavín du Huántar 11th October

An uneasy night for me. Juana repeatedly wound her rope around those bushes and had to be disentangled four times. (The ground was anti picket.) Today the limp is so bad that eight easy miles took us four and a half hours. Never have I felt so unhappy about an animal and so impatient to arrive at a destination. We rejoiced in mid-afternoon to find ourselves overlooking Chavín at the base of a massive mountain, its red-tiled roofs straggling for a mile or so between river and cliffs and many fields of alfalfa visible around the edges.

A young policeman helped us to find a burly *mestizo* veterinario who after a superficial examination said Juana needs only a few days' rest – which is nonsense. Tomorrow we'll consult the alternative who is 'out of town' today. Juana is now safely corralled behind a little building in which the town's electricity is (or not, as the case may be) generated. The two men in charge have advised us to soak her feet in *aguarrás* (turps) twice a day. And one of them left his post to show us a tiny shop down a side street where we could buy this medicament. Chavín is at 9,500 feet with a perfect climate and hot sulphur springs nearby. We can think of nowhere more congenial for a rest-halt of indefinite length.

25th October

We'll be sad to leave tomorrow, after fifteen days in welcoming Chavín. The second vet, Foro, assured us that Juana's legs were sound but, despite frequent consultations, he took five days to diagnose a foot abscess. Then he hastened off to borrow a butcher's saw and I held Juana for seventeen long minutes while he penetrated through her hoof, all the time making soothing Quechua noises. He remarked on the patient's strange docility and we agreed that animals usually know when they are being 'hurt to help'. But towards the end she reared a few times, pawing the air. About a pint of vile pus was followed by water and blood. At home she would have been given high-powered antibiotic injections; here she was given a perfunctory wipe with a dirty damp cloth. Next morning she looked happier than she had done for a fortnight.

Three days later there was no trace of a limp. Foro advised shoeing and 150 soles bought a set of shoes from our dosshouse proprietor; hot-shoeing is unknown here. By noon a curious crowd had gathered to observe our mini-drama and the neighbourhood baker, by now a good friend of ours, helped me to hold Juana's head. Foro and his amigo the cloth merchant – Sinchi, who had closed shop for the occasion – held her legs. During hind feet shoeing, the relevant leg was tied to a rope that had already been firmly knotted to her tail: an ingenious kick-inhibiting device. On the whole she behaved well, considering how bewildering and alarming this experience must have been; only once did she seriously attempt to escape. We were concerned to see her wincing as the nails entered the injured hoof but Foro thought this of no significance; naturally that foot would remain sensitive for some time. At that point Rachel decided to ride no more, to walk the remaining nine hundred or so miles to Cuzco. We are rejoicing to see our *mula* again looking so *bonita*; she has regained most of her lost weight (unlike us). But of course she looked puzzled and miserable as she took her first shod steps – why did the ground suddenly feel so odd…?

Camp on wet ledge of High Mountain 26th October

Juana stepped out smartly today, already adjusted to her new footwear. The path to La Union runs slightly south of east across this Cerro de Vincos *puna* – a high, treeless plateau – or so I presume. The map is unhelpful but our Chavín friends firmly believe in a little-used trail.

The sun shone warm this morning but by noon dark clouds were crouching coldly on nearby crests as we traversed a massive rock wall with a sheer drop into a tree-filled canyon. Soon this tricky path caused some apprehension because of our new-shod Juana. The rain started as we reached the more or less level puna and quickly the path became a mud rink. We all found it hard to remain upright and here for the first time Juana slipped, went over on her side and for a moment lay floundering. As we helped her to her feet Rachel stated the obvious – 'Lucky this didn't happen on the way up!'

It began to snow as our path rose still higher, taking us around the shoulder of a craggy mountain to a wide ledge with, mercifully, ample grazing. By getting the tent up as quickly as numbed fingers permitted, we contrived to keep our night gear dry.

Casa on Puna 27th October

At 7.30 a.m. we moved off and some five hours later we were overlooking a broad green valley, very far below. Descending, our faint path took us to the base of a ferocious jumble of rock peaks; even by the standards to which we have become adjusted, it seemed absurd to expect any path to cross that wall. Sometimes Juana prudently refused stretches of bare rock, feasible for me but in her estimation suggesting a death-trap. Three times we were forced to descend hundreds of feet and start again in our quest for a mule-friendly way over a particularly dangerous bit. Juana's choices were atrociously dangerous in my view, of iced mud and preternaturally steep. But she much preferred them to rock slabs. Meanwhile Rachel had sensibly abandoned us and was finding her own way up by a route that from a distance looked more suited to an ibex than a biped.

This evening Rachel asked why we both felt so tired when today's distances and altitudes were not exceptional. I theorised, in my unscientific way, that the extreme cold, and being wet through, demanded an abnormal amount of energy to generate the heat necessary for survival.

Jauja 12th November

In this town, an important market centre since pre-Inca days, we set out on a serious shopping expedition. Rachel had pointed out that my jeans are in a state of disrepair beyond the bounds of decency...

To celebrate my augmented wardrobe we had *café con leche* in a large restaurant near the Mercado. At the next table six silent men were drinking hard and frequently peeing, with astonishing accuracy, into a circular hole in the floor which lacked even a token enclosing wall. I like people to be uninhibited about their natural functions but this seemed to be going a little far.

Jauja 16th November

Today we hogged Juana's mane and Rachel groomed her to brilliance. Afterwards our new friend Domingo remarked that if we sold her here we could buy a sturdy pony for half the price fetched for an elegant mula. His eyes twinkled when I reacted rather as though he'd suggested I should sell Rachel. Not only do we love Juana but she – God knows why! – loves us. Even when fodder is not an issue she follows me around and on hearing our voices from a distance she greets us delightedly. One can't exchange animals as though they were mere motor cars. And Domingo would, I suspect, have been quite shocked if we had acted on his suggestion.

Cuzco 20th December

The Cuzco Tourist Office organises pony-trekking during the dry season. At home no-one would condemn a beloved animal to such a career; here, one-day treks with a long rainy season vacation offer an easier life than regularly carrying loads to market and pulling primitive ploughs up precipices. So we asked Sancho, the tourist office in-charge, if he would like to buy a beautiful, intelligent and hardy young mula. His father, he said, is the expert – and he locked up the office and we all set off for his nearby home where a sharp-eyed mother looked contemptuously at our beloved and snapped – '*Muy flaca!*' (Very lean) which, alas, is true. But father approved and we settled on 27,000 soles.

Cuzco 21st December

We spent most of today with Sancho, commuting between the District Police Headquarters (as in Cajamarca, the police had to be deeply involved) and the office of the Public Notary where for hours everyone ignored us. When all four certificates had been stamped three times by different clerks, we set off for Sancho's home – and there got a shock. Already Juana had been moved (by goods train) to an uncle's pasture down the Urubamba Valley, 'because now in the rains there are no riding tourists and she needs to get fat.' After the first horrid moment we were glad. Not saying goodbye is always much easier.

The Irish author **Dervla Murphy** is one of the most distinguished writers on travel in English. Her twenty-six books all bear the Murphy hallmark of rejecting all comforts and seeking genuine interaction with the people, landscape and politics of the remote areas she travels through. As a post  script to the above extract she writes: 'In the forty years since the book was written I have received many letters (cc. NSPCC, RSPCA) deploring my selfish cruelty. Interestingly, as the decades pass the complaints become more strident. In twenty-first-century playgrounds, Affluent World children are provided with soft surfaces on which to fall. How soon will this sub-species become extinct?'

Barry's Flying Visit

Adrian Phillips

When did Barry first enter my life? Let me think. Well, he may have been with our group when Fredy led us into the swamp on the hunt for anacondas. Or when we took that night walk through the grasping foliage and Fredy had to rescue us all from the herd of wild pigs. Yes, perhaps he was there then. But perhaps not. The truth is I've no idea now. That's the rainforest for you; it can hypnotise a callow tourist with flurrying parakeets and howler monkeys booming from misty treetops so that time becomes nothing but a series of vivid moments, like bulb flashes at the backs of your eyes.

Let's just say we came together at some point during that four-day expedition, and for a while we were inseparable. We remained together on the river journey back out of the jungle and on the flight home to the UK. I took him on walks around my local haunts, on evenings out in town, and to the Cotswolds when I visited my mother over the bank holiday weekend. He even shared my bed.

And then, on a Saturday morning, as I sat dreaming in a chair, Barry poked his head out of my leg.

If you've ever been dreaming in a chair when something pokes its head out of your leg, you'll know it's the oddest experience. I should clarify: this wasn't like a scene in *Alien* when a slimy thing that's more teeth than anything else bursts from the body of an unsuspecting astronaut, and everyone's popcorn goes flying. Barry's emergence was really a graceful flick, quickly out and in, so fast that I initially assumed it a trick of the light. But, no, there he came again, a little worming tentacle appearing from the centre of an inflamed insect bite on my thigh. I found the performance ghoulishly fascinating. It didn't hurt; the pleasure of witnessing my wife's horrified expression would have compensated for a great deal of discomfort in any case.

Having said that, I wasn't overly keen on Barry becoming a long-term resident. For minutes on end he would remain out of sight, like a soldier under sniper fire, and the knowledge of him hunkered down somewhere beneath my skin, living and pulsing, made me itch all over. I knew he must be a rainforest parasite. Fredy had entertained us one evening with stories of parasitic larvae as we ate a dinner of piranha on the floor of his hut. He even described his favoured method of extraction. 'I make a special noise until the worm pops up,' he had explained, 'and then spit tobacco juice on it. The worm gets drunk' – at this point he had rolled his eyes in imitation of an inebriated worm – 'and you can grab it!'

Oh that Fredy were with me now. I didn't have any tobacco juice to hand. Even if I had, I couldn't remember the special noise. There was nothing for it but to seek advice closer to home, so I phoned the travel pharmacy on the high street.

'Good morning, I wonder whether you can help. I recently returned from Ecuador and I've just noticed something moving in my leg.'

'Sorry, say again? I thought you said *moving* in your *leg*.'

It became quickly evident that the removal of worms from legs wasn't an area of expertise for the lady at the travel pharmacy on the high street.

'Yes, that's right. It's white.'

'Ah, OK. Hmmm. Would you hold the line for a moment?'

There followed some urgent, muffled conversation with a fellow expert behind the desk at the travel pharmacy on the high street. A minute later, she was back.

'Hello? Thanks for holding. I've consulted with my colleague, and we both agree that you should go to the hospital immediately'.

'You don't have an ointment or something?'

'Errm, no.'

'And it's probably best not just to leave it?'

'No, probably best not.'

'Righto, thanks anyway.'

'No problem at all. Goodbye.' Then, before the receiver hit the cradle, I heard her say 'That's *disgus-*'. My sense was that she was addressing her colleague rather than me.

It was on the drive to hospital that I christened my parasite 'Barry'. It felt right to give him a name, seeing as we were existing so intimately. But more than that, in an unexpected emotional development that doubtless a psychologist could explain, perhaps by pointing to studies of Stockholm syndrome, I was beginning to feel a certain affection for the tiny chap. He'd come a long way. I admired his pluck. And, after all, he'd chosen my thigh over several others among our party; there was something gratifying about that, like being picked first for a school team.

Humankind was well represented in the waiting room of Northwick Park Hospital. It largely looked pretty glum, rows of faces staring into space beneath a whiteboard reminding them that the current waiting time was at least 180 minutes. I registered at the front desk, and then wedged myself between an old lady with her arm in a sling and a man with his eyes closed and a grubby T-shirt riding high up his doughy stomach.

'Don't expect to be seen quickly, dear' said the old woman conversationally. 'I've been here two hours now, and – '

'*Adrian? Adrian Phillips?*' called a nurse with a clipboard and immaculate eyebrows. 'Come with me, please.'

I got up and made a sheepish exit past hundreds of outraged eyes. News of the case of the bloke with something living in his leg had obviously spread quickly among the hospital staff. Barry had star factor, and you don't keep a star waiting among the common herd.

I was led down the corridor to a cubicle through a gaggle of curious junior doctors. 'Shoo, shoo!' said the nurse, wafting them away and closing the door behind us. 'That's better. Now, my name's Bob. What do we have here?'

My working theory – based on some internet searches on my phone – was that Barry was a sand flea or 'jigger'. Jiggers, I learnt, lurk about in sandy soil until an unsuspecting host comes along. They then hop on, burrow headfirst beneath the skin, and generally set about making themselves at home, feeding on blood and posting their bodily excretions out of the hole.

I lay on the bed in my boxer shorts as Bob peered at my leg. The area in question certainly resembled images of sand flea infestations I'd found online: a reddish lump – or, to use the correct term, a 'warble' – with a dot of deepest black at its centre that would occasionally contract or dilate as the creature fidgeted inside. There were some nagging doubts, though. For one, sand fleas aren't good jumpers, and so all the examples I'd found were on people's feet rather than their thighs. And I hadn't come across any reference to a white tentacle. But Bob wasn't a man to let nagging doubts get in the way of making a name for himself along the corridors of Northwick Park Hospital, and so after Googling various descriptions of how to remove jiggers, and watching a short video of a tribesman cutting a jigger out of his own toe with a thorn, he gathered his instruments and got to work.

Initially, Bob favoured the waiting game. He sat staring intensely at the warble, motionless, a pair of tweezers poised in front of his face in anticipation of Barry's appearance; he reminded me of a heron about to strike. Barry, however, had become uncharacteristically shy – he wasn't stupid. And Bob wasn't really the patient type. After a while, he started pecking lightly at the hole with the tweezers, perhaps hoping Barry would pop up to see what all the commotion was about.

As it became clear that waiting and pecking weren't working, Bob elected for more forceful action. 'This might sting a bit,' he warned, as he made several injections of anaesthetic around the lump, and began squeezing it between his thumbs. My eyes watered and the warble grew redder, the skin webbed with broken veins as Bob pressed harder and harder. Still no Barry.

Bob considered things for a moment before rummaging through a drawer and producing an oversized needle with a hook at the end. This was Bob's big push, his all or nothing bid for glory. He crouched over my leg, picking and digging and squeezing as I winced at the ceiling. The hole was widening, filling with blood that he dabbed away with a scrap of white muslin. He continued for 15 minutes in this way, working with the relish of the Merchant of Venice claiming his pound of flesh, until the cloth was mottled red. Finally he stopped and gazed down dumbly at his handiwork; the tip of his little finger could have fitted inside the wound he'd created. 'I don't think it's coming out,' he admitted weakly, his face pale, and then retreated to confess to his boss.

Barry would have enjoyed our trip to the Hospital of Tropical Diseases the next day because Fitzrovia wasn't a part of town he'd seen before. His celebrity status, though, was very much diminished. The staff there weren't to be wowed by a mere sand flea, and we waited for over two hours as they called a string of patients to cubicles to test for leishmaniasis and schistosomiasis and any number of other maladies ending in 'sis'.

When my turn did arrive, it came with a couple of bombshells. First, and not entirely a surprise, was the news that – even when tobacco juice was in short supply – Bob's approach was not recommended best practice for the treatment of parasites. 'I'm horrified,' said the consultant after she had removed the dressing from my thigh. 'A botfly larva should be teased out carefully!' And therein lay the second bombshell. Barry was a botfly not a jigger.

She showed me a photo of a botfly larva, plump and anaemic, with hairs on its segmented body and a breathing tube protruding from its backside, which is what I had thought was its head squirming out of my thigh. When a botfly egg comes into contact with skin, the larva hatches and eats its way into the host with sharp black fangs, gorging and growing to over an inch in length before exiting a few weeks later to complete its transformation into a fly. It's an animal that only a parent could love.

But you had to admit that 'Barry the botfly' was pleasingly alliterative, I thought, smiling to myself. It seemed meant to be. I only hoped Barry could forgive me for mistaking his arse for his face.

'They've almost certainly killed it,' said the consultant, bringing me back abruptly to the matter in hand. 'We can't leave the body in there. You'll need an operation.'

No trace of Barry was ever found. The official verdict was that he'd been squished between Bob's thumbs and his juices absorbed by my body. But I prefer to believe he somehow made his escape when Bob's back was turned, ghosting out of my life just as he'd ghosted into it. There's a nice symmetry to that; it's almost poetic. The surgeon at University College London Hospital cut out an area two inches long and an inch wide in his search for any pieces of Barry, and the wound was left to heal naturally rather than stitched because of the risk of infection. It's an impressive scar. I'll show you some time.

A couple of months later, I met Fredy in a pub on the Strand. His rainforest tourism project had been shortlisted for an award, and he'd flown across to attend a swanky champagne ceremony at the Savoy Hotel. I'd never seen anyone so out of place in a suit. We reminisced about my stint in the jungle, and laughed at the memory of being chased up that tree by the wild pigs. Of course, I couldn't wait to tell him about Barry, and he listened to my story with chin propped in his leathered hand and brow furrowed in concentration. When I'd finished, he was silent for a while. And then, with a puzzled shake of the head, he asked 'Why didn't you try the special noise?'

Adrian Phillips is MD of Bradt Travel Guides, and an award-winning travel writer/broadcaster for national media outlets including *The Telegraph*, *The Guardian*, *The Independent*, *National Geographic Traveller* and the BBC. Barry wasn't the only parasite Adrian picked up during his short stay in Ecuador – he was also diagnosed with an amoeba in his bloodstream. But that's another story.

Pepper Pays her Passage

Celia Dillow

'Boys, how would you like to pack your things, leave your friends and move to the other side of the world?' we asked, brightly.

'Is Pepper going too?' was their first thought.

'But… of course she is!' My husband and I glanced at each other.

Actually, it is not impossible to take a bearded collie to Argentina. It is not impossible, but it is complicated. And very expensive.

'Why not rehome her?' was a common question from well-meaning friends and family. 'There are plenty of dogs in Argentina…'

'For the cost of her air fare we could buy five new ones,' I heard my husband rumble softly.

However, for this journey taking the dog was the deal breaker. She was the first one the boys thought about when they woke up in the morning and the last they kissed goodnight before they went to sleep. She was part of the pack.

Ten days before departure, I called the airline and:

'Si, Signora, we know you are travelling with your dog and she is booked from Rome to Buenos Aires.'

'But we are travelling from London, sir.'

'Yes, but the plane from London is too small – you just need to get her to Rome.'

It was the week before Christmas, my life was in packing cases, my heart was breaking and my sense of humour had been missing for weeks. Friends stepped in. They gently led Pepper away and left me dry-eyed and rocking in the corner. I was worried she might not survive the journey; she could die of stress or heat exhaustion or hypothermia. I googled stories of owners collecting boxes of dead pets from the airport.

But, a couple of weeks later, Pepper made her first solo flight. In proper diva style, she delayed the British Airways flight on the runway while her sky kennel was adjusted. Twenty-four hours later, anxious at the other end, we visited various men behind airport desks and paid a series of 'taxes' to get her released. And then she was unceremoniously brought across the scrubby tarmac on a forklift and dumped. The boys broke open the kennel and grabbed her through the fence.

Pepper did not know she had just flown across the world, of course. What do dogs understand about journeys? So there was little adjustment on her part. For a highly strung collie, she made very little fuss. She soon got used to her claws skittering on the tiled floors in the house and found the shadiest places to lie. Perhaps the birds called in a different language, but she did not need to learn it. The raucous call of the rufous hornero, Argentina's emblematic ovenbird, always sent her charging into the garden; she learnt to return around the edge of the lawn to avoid the prickly thistle grass. She never got used to the wire mosquito panels around the terrace, however, and crashed through them many times.

The school where we lived and worked looked like an English public school. Built at the end of the nineteenth century, it had strong British connections. There was a fine campus of rugby pitches, tennis courts and swimming pools. But the sky was blue for three hundred days a year, summers were hot and the winters were mild. Leggy southern lapwings viciously guarded their nests on the outfields and flew at Pepper if she got too close. Vultures and caracara hawks tipped and tilted in the warm air. The school buildings were cloaked in white jasmine and bougainvillea, and poinsettia grew as large as trees. Our house was a hundred years old with tall shuttered windows and a cool, tiled terrace wrapped around the back. It sat at the top of a steep bank and looked out across the floodplain towards the Rio de la Plata. Toads, the size of dinner plates, lived in the drains under the house and sang long and loud into the hot southern night. I often had to turn them out of the cricket bags and helmets in the porch. Lime-green parakeets shrieked in the palm trees outside the bedrooms; hummingbirds buzzed and feasted from the lavender and rosemary around the windows.

Pepper's favourite spot was on top of the bank, face to the wind, barking her presence to the *barrio*. There were always dogs barking. It was a noisy place. Trolley buses clattered past in a conversation-stopping cloud. There were whistles, tannoys, sirens, horns and bells; chapel clock, school bells, bicycle bells and wind chimes. As she sat on her bank, did she notice that the air was different? Argentina smells like heaven for dogs. Logs burn slowly on *parilla* grills, and there is always the scent of roasting meat. Soon thoroughly at home, Pepper became a familiar spectator at rugby and cricket and hockey. She joined in the school's sponsored walks and the annual steeplechase and carol-singing events. The boarders, some a thousand miles from home and missing their own pets, loved to play with her, although we often had to explain her name. To their ears, it sounded as if we had named our dog Pee-pee!

As the seasons changed, storms rumbled up the river and cracked overhead for twenty-four hours at a time. The sun would rise reluctantly and the campus would drip under a torrent of rain. Usually,

Pepper burrowed into the back of the wardrobe and sat tight until it was over. But on one eerie, acid-yellow morning, she bolted.

We went out with torches and wellies, calling. By breakfast time the boys were hoarse and sobbing. I sent them to school but they all found excuses to pop home, asking breathlessly, 'Is she back yet?' Later in the morning I joined the search party as we scoured the school site. All the ground staff were looking for her. Touchingly, the head of maintenance drove around the blocks outside the school walls and into the shanty town, calling and calling.

During the afternoon, as the storm crashed back across the pampa, I went out again, swinging her lead, repeating all our usual routes. She trotted out from the tractor sheds, shook herself vigorously and smiled. Back at home, I pulled her to me and buried my face in her pewter-and-pearls fur. 'Don't leave me,' I wept. 'Please, don't leave me.'

Pepper's assimilation was simple. We, on the other hand, made very different journeys. We had to learn how to live and walk and talk again. We were lonely and homesick. We had to build a life in another language: attend school, play cricket, make friends; buy school uniforms, go to meetings, open bank accounts and do business. Often, I was spitting with frustration because I could only talk like a toddler. But Pep was there too, unendingly jolly, never judgemental and easy to talk to.

Out and about, she was a talking point and our vocabulary grew in unusual directions. '*Es un collie barbudo*,' we learnt to explain. Passers-by would stop to take her picture. Questions ranged from the expected, 'What is she?' and 'Where does she come from?' to the frankly strange, 'Does your dog have eyes?' Before trips to the vet or the groomer, I gritted my teeth and looked up the unusual bits and pieces of language that I needed. The man in the pet shop said he would shear her for me.

I went through to the back of his shop and he rapidly removed her coat, chatting amiably about the British government's wrong-headed policy in the Falkland Islands. He was armed with scissors and sharp blades while I had only my faltering Spanish to defend Her Majesty's honour, and so I kept quiet. Pepper emerged looking like a whippet, but she was cool for the summer.

As we found our feet, we became eager for adventure. With Pepper curled into the tiniest space in the back of the car, we zig-zagged across that vast land. She walked with us in the Andes and swam in the South Atlantic. At the beach she kept cool by digging herself a hole in the endless white dunes. In the water, gin-clear and cold as ice, she barked as the waves knocked us down and filled our pants with sand. Further along the coast we parked at the famous harbour in Mar del Plata and took Pepper to look over the wall. She bounced up and recoiled in shock. I watched as she tested the air. What was that smell? The enormous male sea lions were hauled out on the jetty. She tried to fit them into her idea of the world. Furry not-dogs? Barking fish? Fish dogs?

There were encounters with other creatures, too. In the ancient granite of the Sierras de Tandil, we went to walk in the soft autumn air. She looked perplexed as an armadillo trundled around the car park looking for picnic scraps. And as we headed into the hills she blithely stepped over a basking rattlesnake; we all did. At camp that week she spent a lot of time rolling on the burrows of the owls. The little diurnal owls sat on the fence posts and blinked in surprise. She was with us when we saw our first condor, on the twisting roads of the Central Sierras. A juvenile drifted above the track; it was so close we could hear the wind trembling through its mighty primaries. Later, she was keen to scramble up the rocks and chase the boys across the scree, but she could barely move the next day. We thought we had broken her. She limped after us as we collected pine cones for the fire and then cuddled up in a tiny cabin under a huge harvest moon. We took it in turns to massage her back. She did not complain.

Pepper played a vital role within her pack and she helped us to feel normal when our lives were turned upside down and nothing was recognisable anymore. And so her adventures with us continued when we moved to Italy, another land that is fragrant with food. She swapped her shady spot in the garden for a roof terrace with a view of the Alps. She learnt that the Italian dogs that live in apartments are usually grumpy and that pizza crusts are always delicious. And every school holiday, when we drove home through the mountains, up the edge of Germany and across northern France, she curled into the tiniest space in the car, surrounded by olive oil, balsamic vinegar, cheese and wine. She never complained. She did not move until she was able to jump out and sniff the air of our Somerset home, and then she patiently trotted into the garden, and barked her presence to the village.

It is not easy to take a bearded collie on an adventure. It is not easy, but it is possible and I am so very glad we did. She is forever in our story-box of memories. The journeys would not have been the same without her. Over the years, I watched everyone, in turn, bury their faces in her soft fur and tell her how rubbish the world was or how much it hurt or how they missed their cool, green, misty home. She definitely earned her passage.

Celia Dillow spent five years in South America. It changed everything. Now settled in southwest Britain, she reads and writes about the magic and mystery of those faraway southern lands. She is a specialist dyslexia teacher during term time and a traveller, writer, birdwatcher and hiker during the holidays.

Just a Dog

Emma Laing

Our first night at the Cuban resort, my boyfriend Julian and I had set out to explore the neighbourhood. The evening was warm and sticky and we'd sat on a bench to rest. We didn't notice a blur of white, black and tan streak across the road until it landed directly in my lap. A gorgeous, soft, sweet-smelling, foxy-faced puppy with the hugest, most adorable ears I'd ever seen looked up into my eyes, licked my chin and then snuggled into my lap as if she planned to stay.

I fell for her in that second. The fact she followed us to the hotel, participated wholeheartedly in our plan to sneak her into our room and stayed with us for five days just compounded my attachment.

When not staying with us, she seemed to be out foraging for food. She was skinny, but not badly undernourished, and the fact she had no collar, and that she was alone on the street after 11 p.m., led us to conclude she was a stray.

Those five days were spent on the palm tree-fringed beach under a perfect blue sky with Lily sleeping in the shade of our sunbeds. When I retrieved a drink from the beach bar or a snack from the café she would wake and pad after me. Mealtimes were a challenge. Although no-one had reprimanded us for having a dog in the hotel grounds, we couldn't exactly bring her into the dining room. There was a grassy area outside so I'd tell her to stay there and she'd sit, seemingly content to wait. We didn't adopt her, she adopted us.

So was it any wonder, when it was time to go home, I felt my heart was being wrenched in two? The voices of reason insisted we couldn't take her with us. *We don't know the rules about taking a dog out of the island. It's a ridiculous idea, Emma. You need to get over it!*

We flew back to our home in Bogota, but I couldn't stop thinking of that little Cuban *perrita*, wondering where she was and hoping she was safe. When I returned to my teaching job, I contemplated whether she would still be trotting up and down that same road.

Why couldn't I let this go? I tried to get over it, really I did. I knew she was *just a dog* and told myself not to be so melodramatic. But once she'd got her dainty black-and-white claws into my heart, she wouldn't let go.

I googled for information about adopting Cuban dogs. Turned out it wasn't quite so crazy after all. Or at least, there were lots of other crazies like me. I emailed a girl at our hotel who was willing to look out for Lily and said she'd seen her the day before. But that was followed by weeks of no news and it became clear the only way to be sure was to return to Cuba and look for her myself.

At the end of my tether, I confided in a friend, expecting him to say, 'Emma, this is insane. Just get another dog!' But against all odds he asked, 'Why not go back? See if you can find her and if you can't, have another holiday!'

Julian had a different perspective. 'What if you don't find her? Imagine how disappointed you'll be.' He was right, I knew. But I also realised I couldn't move past this until I'd given it my best shot. If it meant doing something a little irrational, then so be it. I firmly believe a bit of crazy is sometimes necessary to survive in life.

So, with my holiday allowance already spent, I quit my job and booked a flight. Along with most resources for animals, and many for humans, dog crates were scarce in Cuba so I brought a big empty one with me.

I asked around the neighbourhood, showing photos. I rode a tourist train the length of the Varadero Peninsula, peering out the back eagerly. I hired a bike and cycled the small streets and paths. I waited on the white sands at sunrise and walked up and down the tree-lined road at night, calling her name. I printed posters with Lily's photo, offering a reward for news of her whereabouts, and taped them to telegraph poles all over town. But after six days of searching, not a white tail nor a pair of tall, tan-coloured ears had been glimpsed.

The street dogs rested in the shade during the hottest part of the day, so I'd wait until after dinner for a final search. In the meantime, I might as well make the most of the free bar on my last day. My heart was heavy, but I'd done my best. I sipped a cold beer and wondered how I was going to return to Bogota the next day and face Julian, having failed in my mission.

'*Señora!*' The girl on reception was looking at me and holding out the phone.

'*Hola, es* Emma?' a female voice asked. '*Mi amigo tiene la perrita.* Lily.'

A rush of optimism surged through me, but I tried to remain calm, breathing deeply before asking if she was sure it was Lily. She sounded convinced and I allowed myself a glimmer of hope, arranging to meet that evening.

The next four hours were interminable. I tried to sunbathe, I tried to read, but my brain kept on nagging. *Would it be Lily?* I needed to distract myself with action so I returned to my room to pack.

When the hour of reckoning finally came, I sat on a step outside reception studying photos of Lily on my phone, focusing on something to distinguish her from any other similar-sized stray with black, white and tan colouring. I committed her most striking characteristics to memory: the almond eyes lined with what looked like thick black kohl, the white line running the length of her snout and, of course, those huge adorable ears.

A flicker of movement caught my eye and I looked up. A couple were walking towards the hotel, followed by a small, foxy-looking dog. A black-and-white-and-tan-coloured dog with unexpectedly large pointed ears. The dog looked up from whatever olfactory delight had attracted its interest and gazed over with those dramatic dark eyes.

'Lily!'

I scrambled to my feet. She looked directly at me and without a second's hesitation darted across the empty street. I crouched to greet her.

'Oh, Lily! *Hola, mi perrita.*'

She jumped up, paws on my chest, and licked my face enthusiastically, her whole body swaying in rhythm with her furiously wagging tail. I stroked her soft coat and studied her thoroughly. There was no doubt in my mind, or my heart, that this was our long-lost furry friend.

I thanked the couple profusely and gladly paid the reward. Now I had Lily and my flight was tomorrow afternoon. Fortunately, I'd made contact with a local vet, so the first thing to do was take a taxi to her practice. The diminutive Gladis opened the door and didn't waste a second in assessing Lily's condition. She agreed with my estimate that Lily was around eight months old and informed me she was in heat. That would make her trip to Bogota all the more stressful. She told me Lily needed to see the department vet first thing tomorrow.

At 7.30 a.m. the following day, we were ushered into the stark examination room. Lily was subjected to a swift but thorough check-up. Her ears dropped to half-mast and her long white tail followed suit. Half an hour later, armed with the relevant documents and a somewhat harassed but officially sanctioned *perrita*, the real journey began.

Lily stuck her head out of the window and sniffed the air.

Carlos, our taxi driver, turned around and flashed us a warm smile. '*El aeropuerto, sí?*'

He turned the radio up and I settled into the back seat. Lily, however, couldn't stay still. She pattered across me, switching from one side to the other.

After twenty minutes of constant movement, she finally sat still on my lap with her head pointed towards the footwell. Perhaps she wanted to curl up down there and sleep. I let her move forward, but she remained on my lap and her body convulsed. *Uh-oh*! She was about to puke. I looked around wildly for a receptacle and grabbed my hat, managing to position it in front of her nose just in time.

She looked decidedly down in the mouth after that and curled up quietly on the back seat. I thanked the powers that be I'd brought a hat.

Our next mission was to pick up the *guacal*, or crate, that Lily would stay in during the flight. Taking that empty box back would have been the saddest of sights, but now I had a canine companion who would soon be taking up residence.

Two hours before our flight I checked in. I'd reserved a place for Lily when I booked so they were expecting her.

'*Señora?*' A voice at my shoulder made me jump. Lily and I looked into the serious face of an airport official. The man shook my hand briefly, not making eye contact. He consulted his clipboard, running a hand over Lily's flank. She wagged her tail cautiously. The official was content that Lily and her documents conformed to regulations. I gave silent thanks and prepared for our departure.

A sinking feeling descended to the pit of my stomach and the air seemed too thick. I wished I could take her inside the cabin, not leave her alone in the hold, but she was too big to fit under the seat. Only cats or chihuahuas could squeeze under there. I encouraged her back into the guacal.

'Time to go now, little one.' I stroked her head. She looked up at me and licked my chin.

I rolled the trolley towards the oversized luggage point and lifted the crate on to the conveyor belt that would carry her off to the inner realm. The paper tag bearing her name was affixed to the handle. I hoped a sympathetic luggage handler might soothe her with a kind word. Lily was sitting, one ear up, one ear down, looking at me with anxious, questioning eyes. My own eyes blurred and I told myself to get a grip. Finding her had been the hardest part; now we just needed to fly home.

'Bye, sweetheart, see you soon.' I waved and walked away blindly towards security.

The short flight seemed never-ending. My mind kept returning to that little pup stashed among the suitcases, eyes wide, flinching over every noise and bump. Finally, we made a bouncy arrival at Bogota El Dorado. I wanted to run and check on Lily right away, but airport procedure had to be followed. After a mercifully brief wait at immigration, I made it to the oversized luggage window.

The curtain flapped back and Lily's crate was lifted out on to the wide ledge in front of me. There was no sound or movement from inside. Heart thumping, I went to the door end and looked inside. There she was, lying right at the back with eyes wide.

'*Hola*, Lily!' Relief flooded through me. She was probably in shock after her ordeal, but she was safe now and soon she'd be home. Once we got through customs, of course. Despite weeks of indecision and longing, days of helpless searching and walking the streets, followed by hours of frantic activity, we had finally made it. From Cuba to Colombia, Lily was here and the next chapter of her life was about to begin.

Emma Laing is a communications professional from Jersey in the Channel Islands who now lives in Bogota with her Colombian partner. They have recently opened a micropub, called The Cider House, the first and only bar to specialise in cider in Latin America. Emma spends her spare time travelling and writing.

From *The Whispering Land*

Gerald Durrell

Gerald Durrell spent eight months travelling in Argentina in the late 1950s, collecting animals for his then recently founded Jersey Zoo. Along windswept Patagonian shores and in tropical forests, he was drawn to rare and interesting creatures which he hoped would thrive and breed in captivity.

When you have a large collection of animals to transport from one end of the world to the other you cannot, as a lot of people seem to think, just hoist them aboard the nearest ship and set off with a gay wave of your hand. There is slightly more to it than this. Your first problem is to find a shipping company who will agree to carry animals. Most shipping people, when you mention the words 'animal cargo' to them, grow pale, and get vivid mental pictures of the Captain being eviscerated on the bridge by a jaguar, the First Officer being slowly crushed in the coils of some enormous snake, while the passengers are pursued from one end of the ship to the other by a host of repulsive and deadly beasts of various species. Shipping people, on the whole, seem to be under the impression you want to travel on one of their ships for the sole purpose of releasing all the creatures which you have spent six hard months collecting.

Once, however, you have surmounted this psychological hurdle, there are still many problems. There are consultations with the Chief Steward as to how much refrigeration space you can have for your meat, fish and eggs, without starving the passengers in consequence; the Chief Officer and the Bosun have to be consulted on where and how your cages are to be stacked, and how they are to be secured for rough weather, and how many ship's tarpaulins you can borrow. Then you pay a formal call on the Captain and, generally over a gin, you tell him (almost with tears in your eyes) you will be so little trouble aboard that he won't even notice you are there – a statement which neither he nor you believe.

A ship had been procured, consultations with the people on board had been satisfactory, food for the animals had been ordered, and everything appeared to be running smoothly. It was at this precise juncture that Juanita, the baby peccary, decided to liven up life for us by catching pneumonia. The animals were now in a huge shed which had no heating. While this did not appear to worry any of the other animals unduly (although it was the beginning of the Argentine winter and getting progressively colder) Juanita decided to be different. Without so much as a preliminary cough to warn us, Juanita succumbed. In the morning she was full of beans, and devoured her food avidly; in the evening, when we went to cover the animals for the night, she looked decidedly queer. She was, for one thing, *leaning* against the side of her box as if for support, her eyes half-closed, her breathing rapid and rattling in her throat. Hastily I opened the door of the cage and called her. She made a tremendous effort, stood upright shakily, tottered out of the cage and collapsed into my arms. It was in the best cinematic tradition, but rather frightening. As I held her I could hear her breath wheezing and bubbling in her tiny chest, and her body lay in my arms limp and cold.

In order to husband our rapidly decreasing money supplies two friends in Buenos Aires had rallied round and allowed Sophie and me to stay in their respective flats, in order to save on hotel bills.

I was occupying a camp bed in the flat of one David Jones. At the moment when I discovered Juanita's condition David was with me. As I wrapped her up in my coat I did some rapid thinking. The animal had to have warmth, and plenty of it. But I knew we could not provide it in that great tin barn, even if we lit a bonfire like the Great Fire of London. David had now returned at the double from the Land Rover whence he had gone to get a blanket to wrap the pig in. In one hand he was clasping a half-bottle of brandy.

'This any good?' he enquired, as I swaddled Juanita in the blanket.

'Yes, wonderful. Look, heat a drop of milk on the spirit stove and mix a teaspoonful of brandy with it, will you?'

While David did this, Juanita, almost invisible in her cocoon of blanket and coat, coughed alarmingly. Eventually, the brandy and milk were ready, and I managed to get two spoonfuls down her throat, though it was a hard job, for she was almost unconscious.

'Anything else we can do,' said David hopefully, for, like me, he had grown tremendously fond of the little pig.

'Yes, she's got to have a whacking great shot of penicillin and as much warmth and fresh air as she can get.'

I looked at him hopefully.

'Let's take her back to the flat,' said David, as I had hoped he would. We wasted no more time. The Land Rover sped through the rain-glistening streets at a dangerous pace, and how we arrived at the flat intact was a miracle. While I hurried upstairs with Juanita, David rushed round to Blondie's flat, for there Sophie had our medicine chest with the penicillin and the hypodermic syringes.

I laid the by now completely unconscious Juanita on David's sofa, and, although the flat was warm with the central heating, I turned on the electric fire as well, and then opened all the windows that would not create draughts. David was back in an incredibly short space of time, and rapidly we boiled the hypodermic and then I gave Juanita the biggest shot of penicillin I dared. It was, almost, kill or cure, for I had never used penicillin on a peccary before, and for all I knew they might be allergic to it. Then, for an hour, we sat and watched her. At the end of that time I persuaded myself that her breathing was a little easier, but she was still unconscious and I knew she was a very long way from recovery.

'Look,' said David, when I had listened to Juanita's chest for the fourteen-hundredth time, 'are we doing any good, just sitting here looking at her?'

'No,' I said reluctantly, 'I don't think we'll really see any change for about three or four hours, if then. She's right out at the moment, but I think the brandy has a certain amount to do with that.'

'Well,' said David practically, 'let's go and get something to eat at Olly's.'

By the time we had got back to David's flat I was convinced that we should find Juanita dead. When we went into the living room I gazed at the pile of blankets on the sofa, and had to force myself to go and look. I lifted one corner of the blanket gently and a twinkling dark eye gazed up at me lovingly, while a pink plunger-shaped nose wiffled, and a faint, very faint, grunt of pleasure came from the invalid.

'Good God, she's better,' said David incredulously.

'A bit,' I said cautiously. 'She's not out of danger yet, but I think there's a bit of hope.'

As if to second this Juanita gave another grunt.

In order to make sure that Juanita did not kick off her blanket during the night and make her condition worse I took her to bed with me on the sofa. She lay very quietly across my chest and slept deeply.

Though her breathing was still wheezy it had lost that awful rasping sound which you could hear with each breath she took to begin with.

I was awoken the following morning by a cold, rubbery nose being pushed into my eye, and hearing Juanita's wheezy grunts of greeting. I unwrapped her and saw she was a different animal. Her eyes were bright, her temperature was normal, her breathing was still wheezy, but much more even, and, best of all, she even stood up for a brief, wobbly moment. From then she never looked back. She got better by leaps and bounds, but the better she felt the worse patient she made. As soon as she could walk without falling over every two steps, she insisted on spending the day trotting about the room, and was most indignant because I made her wear a small blanket, safety-pinned under her chin, like a cloak. She ate like a horse, and we showered delicacies on her.

But it was during the nights that I found her particularly trying. She thought this business of sleeping with me a terrific idea, and, flattering though this was, I did not agree. We seemed to have different ideas about the purposes for which one went to bed. I went in order to sleep, while Juanita thought it was the best time of day for a glorious romp.

A baby peccary's tusks and hooves are extremely sharp, and their noses are hard, rubbery and moist, and to have all these three weapons applied to one's anatomy when one is trying to drift off into a peaceful sleep is trying, to put it mildly. Sometimes she would do a kind of porcine tango with her sharp hooves along my stomach and chest, and at other times she would simply chase her tail round and round, until I began to feel like the unfortunate victim in *The Pit and the Pendulum*. She would occasionally break off her little dance in order to come and stick her wet nose into my eye, to see how I was enjoying it. At other times she would become obsessed with the idea that I had, concealed about my person somewhere, a rare delicacy. It may have been truffles for all I know, but whatever it was she could make a thorough search with nose, tusks and hooves, grunting shrilly and peevishly when she couldn't find anything. Round about three a.m. she would sink into a deep, untroubled sleep. Then, at five-thirty, she would take a quick gallop up and down my body to make sure I woke up in good shape. This lasted for four soul-searing nights, until I felt she was sufficiently recovered, and then I banished her to a box at night, to her intense and vocal indignation.

I had only just pulled Juanita round in time, for no sooner was she better than we got a message to say that the ship was ready to leave. I would have hated to have undertaken a voyage with Juanita as sick as she had been, for I am sure she would have died.

Gerald Durrell, OBE, was born in India in 1925. His family returned to England before settling on the island of Corfu. He joined the staff of Whipsnade Park and in 1947 led his first animal-collecting expedition. He made seventy television programmes about

his trips around the world, and wrote thirty-seven books including *My Family and Other Animals*. In 1959 he founded the Jersey Zoological Park, and in 1964 the Jersey Wildlife Preservation Trust. He died in 1995.

Beer and *Burras*

Graham Mackintosh

By some accounts the average man thinks of sex every seven seconds. A jack donkey or *burro* would laugh at such a claim! As I found out, an uncastrated jackass, if it thinks at all, thinks of sex continuously.

The year 1997 was a big one in Baja. In October, the town of Loreto would be celebrating its three hundredth anniversary – the anniversary of the establishment of the first permanent mission in Baja California, and therefore in both Californias. Many people would be heading seven hundred miles down Baja's Highway 1 to join in the party. Ever since the end of a two-year walk around the coast of Baja in the 1980s, I had wanted to hike 'down the middle' of the peninsula visiting the string of remote Dominican, Franciscan and Jesuit missions along the way. How better to celebrate the anniversary than to follow the historic Camino Real to Loreto, walking with a burro?

Where to begin? Certainly the border. Rather than busy San Diego, Tecate, a quieter crossing thirty miles to the east, was perfect. And where better in that town than the famed brewery. I sent them a fax:

'I would like to discuss with you the possibility of Tecate sponsoring my trip by supplying the beer en route. Also, the Tecate brewery beer garden would be a great place to start my journey, entertain the media and say my goodbyes.'

Cervecería Cuauhtémoc Moctezuma, to give them their full title, could not have been more accommodating. They agreed to everything, and supplied a letter telling their outlets to furnish me with all the beer the burro could carry.

With just four days to go before confronting the media, my search for a burro came to an end one night near the town of San Vicente. Accompanied by some Mexican friends, I approached a group of burros. They looked at us and nervously shuffled off into the darkness. One stood his ground. 'That's him,' Miguel, his owner, said. My flashlight picked out the whitish muzzle and eye rings, and the orange glow from his eyes.

I approached slowly with my hand extended. He moved away. His front legs were crudely hobbled together with rope. He managed to hop a few times, then, as if the effort wasn't worth it, he stopped and turned to look at my offered hand. I moved cautiously to his side, out of kicking range, whispering, 'It's OK, it's OK.'

His nose touched my hand, sniffed, and lingered. I felt the bristly hairs and the thick floppy lips that gently smacked on my palm. He was confident and curious and immediately endearing. Within the white muzzle, I fancied I saw a mischievous smile. I ran my hand along his soft, woolly neck and back, and felt there wasn't a vicious bone in his body.

His belly and the inside of his legs were white; most of the rest of him seemed to be a light, almost pinkish brown. A black stripe ran from the top of his neck, along his spine to the tip of his tail; another ran across his shoulders, forming a distinctive cross.

'I shall call him "Misión",' I declared. There was no time for bargaining strategy so I reluctantly parted with the requested $150. As Miguel stuffed the money in his pocket, he asked how long my journey would last. I told him I would be walking over a thousand miles, and on the trail for at least six months.

'I may need more than one burro,' I rather foolishly intimated.

Miguel retorted, 'Misión may need more than one Graham Mackintosh!'

I had travelled with a pack burro for the final four months of my 1980s coastal walk – a sweet, little white gelding. But Misión was a stallion, an uncastrated jack!

The ceremony at the beer garden was a great success. Beer drunk, goodbyes said, I set off with my amigo up into the mountains and down the mission trail – without knowing my burro was on a mission of his own.

My trip coincided with the biggest El Niño on record. On the west coast of the Americas that meant persistent and perhaps unprecedented rain. In spite of the difficulties and dangers posed by the storms, Misión was able to enjoy a rare abundance of water and grazing, especially in the parched Central Desert region of Baja.

He was a good, strong burro that I felt I could control and handle, though Misión had a propensity to collapse fully loaded whenever he deemed the pack too heavy, as he often did, especially after beer pick-ups. He later developed a taste for beer, and became quite excited at the sight of a red can. Since an alcoholic burro would be a disadvantage on my journey, I saved most of it for myself.

And thank God Baja is such a remote place. Blushes spared, his embarrassing tendency to masturbate with his front legs largely went unseen in the empty desert.

Slowly I learned to trust him and let him wander free with his thoughts before loading and unloading. Big mistake. One morning, he heard the far-off call of a female donkey, and was gone. I chased him for two miles. No way could he be caught on foot. Hiding all my gear in the brush, I went in search of a ranch. It took a couple of mounted cowboys to round him up and bring him back.

One of the cowboys – a small, wiry, fierce-looking character that you would not want to cross – always seemed to have a knife in his hand. Whether cutting potatoes, slicing leather, or whittling wood, he held the knife with about the same intensity as a suicidal samurai. I was not sure if he was altogether serious when he waved it in my direction and said that Misión's problem was 'his *cojones*' before adding, 'He would be happier without them.' He volunteered to perform the service for him there and then, but on behalf of my buddy I politely declined his offer.

A few weeks later, at Rancho Miraflores, a rancher wanted to buy my burro or exchange him for a larger trained mule – but I was too attached to be tempted. The disappointed rancher was determined to get one burro out of me, however, so he brought a *burra*, or female, to Misión and I had no choice but to let him loose. Misión rushed over to his blind date, still tied with an open-mouthed, dumbfounded expression frozen on her face. After a few good sniffs, he touched her nose with his – like he was snatching a quick kiss – and that was the end of the foreplay.

With Misión pumping away with his forelegs hanging on each side of her, the female was now 'mouthing' so hard I wasn't sure if she was in ecstasy or agony. A minute later, a seemingly satisfied Misión slid slowly to the ground. The poor shocked burra was still standing, mouth open, eyes bulging.

In my naivete, I thought that was that and I could now get him loaded and go. Well, Misión thought there was more unloading to be done. He mounted her another three times. At last, she closed her inviting mouth. I retied him to the tree and started to load, hoping he'd have some energy left for the trail.

After I'd got the blankets and pads on his back, he was pulling at the rope and signalling his desire to go back for more. The burra looked at the mushrooming resurgence of his passion; her jaw dropped. I had to 'quick release' him again. After he'd finished with number five and showed signs of wishing to go back for number six, I realised my only hope was to get the object of his lust out of sight.

I asked the grinning older *señor* to take her away. Misión half-heartedly tried to follow, but he was securely attached to a tree. Two of the ranchers came over to express admiration and joke about his prowess.

It was a struggle to drag Misión from the ranch. He kept stopping, curling back his lip and braying pitifully for his new love. The sight of any four-legged creature among the sulphur-coloured wildflowers and towering *cardón* cacti by the side of the dusty road was enough to elicit a pathetic bray. He lavished his most solicitous calls on a large brown bull that stared back in astonishment. Twice I made the mistake of letting him graze freely and looked up to see him hurrying back to the ranch.

And that was just the beginning. At another ranch inland from Santa Rosalía it was obvious Jesús, the owner, wanted something from me. It's bad form in Mexico to rush into business matters. I waited, enjoyed coffee, talked about the family.

Before long, Jesús brought over a burra – to 'see how Misión would react'. He reacted predictably, pulling back his lip and trying to uproot the hitching post… and showing other unmistakable signs of profound interest.

After hurriedly returning the nervous-looking female to the corral, Jesús confessed that he was impressed by my burro's stature, stamina and disposition, and declared that he had three burras and no uncastrated male. 'Do you think your burro can help?'

I assured him that although Misión had already had a hard day, he would be delighted to help.

We took him to the corral. However, these burras were not as accommodating. As soon as he got within range, the three burras rejected him forcefully with wild kicking. Misión stood back, watching, and waiting – braying and farting in his excitement. We all laughed uncontrollably. Jesús started to get concerned about his failure to make a move. 'Your burro is afraid,' he said.

'No, no,' I disagreed, 'he is being very intelligent.' Misión followed one of the females and waited for his moment. After she kicked air, he jumped up, and began pumping vigorously. Unable to kick him, the female burra took off around the corral. With his front legs hanging down her sides, Misión ran on his back legs at just the right speed to keep up and keep on doing his thing. In the billowing cloud of dust, they looked like a two-headed, six-legged centaur.

The serviced female was removed so Misión could concentrate on the other two. They also tried to keep their distance and kicked viciously when Misión approached. He was still obviously very eager, but again his passion was tempered with patience. One at a time he repeated his jump-aboard routine, and hung on for dear life as the reluctant ladies took off.

Misión escaped without injury and, judging by the way they had been left mouthing, won the hearts of the burras and the respect of the ranchers who expressed their admiration for this very strong, very savvy burro!

And so it continued all the way down to Loreto where my journey ended. I don't know how many Misión foals we left behind us, but he certainly left his mark.

We picked up our final twenty-four-pack of beer at the Tecate *depósito*. Misión, who thought he had done all the work on the trip, had a Pavlovian reaction to the red cans, every one of which bore the imprint of Cuchama, the sacred mountain rising above the town of Tecate. He deserved his can as much as I did. The six-month trip was over. We had seen it through together. I didn't need more than one strong, courageous, stout-hearted – and very virile – burro… and mercifully Misión didn't need more than one Graham Mackintosh.

But I needed to find him a good new home. For the first time I got on his back and rode him over to an orchard where he remained in happy, hopelessly spoiled retirement, with occasional beers to keep his spirits up, and, more importantly, visits to nearby ranches to entertain the local burras.

Graham Mackintosh was born in London and graduated from Leeds University with a degree in sociology. He is the author of four books on Baja California. Living in San Diego for twenty years, he  became a US citizen in 2004. He continues to head to Baja whenever he can.

Spinny the Sea Cat

Frances Howorth

With the children in boarding school and the feeling that we wanted to do more in life than run a business, my husband Michael and I decided to sell up, buy a yacht and sail around the world. Some might call it a midlife crisis, but to us it was more a question of seizing the moment. The house and most of its contents sold, we moved our remaining worldly goods aboard a sixty-foot ocean-going ketch. Our children were delighted at the thought of adventurous holidays all around the world. Our elderly Burmese cat had just died and, because we had never had a home together without a cat, we decided to find a new kitten.

Spinnaker was a little ball of fluff and fur when she first stepped aboard *Red Hackle*. A pedigree Burmese cat, she had never had time to get used to life in a house and very quickly found her sea legs. When we left England and set sail, 'Spinny' – as she had become known – soon became a true sea cat, making friends in each and every one of the ports we called at.

From the Mediterranean we sailed down the coast of Africa before hopping across to the Canary Islands. With bananas hanging from the back stay, we sailed south again until the butter melted and the trade winds strengthened. It was a sign we should alter course, set the autopilot on a westerly rhumb line and head towards the island of Saint Lucia in the Caribbean.

Where land-based cats hunt mice, our sea-going furry friend hunted fish. She thought nothing of trotting forward along the leeward side of the yacht on a star-studded night as we sailed across the Atlantic, carefully avoiding the sea water crashing over the bow. She would stop just long enough to pick up a fluttering flying fish that had been unfortunate enough to wash up on to our foredeck, and head back to the cockpit. Like all cats, she had to show us how clever she had been and would arrive at the helm, fish still flapping in her mouth as she made that guttural growl animals do when they have caught their prey.

Eighteen days later, we began to smell the sweet aromas of tropical rainforest. Shortly after that, the distinctive outline of the mountain peaks known as the Pitons pierced the horizon and we knew then that our first ever transatlantic sailing voyage in our own boat was nearly over.

Saint Lucia became home for a while, during which time we rested and changed our routine to become cruising sailors. Spinny used her time to develop new skills, chief among which was cockroach hunting. She thought it was hilariously funny to catch the biggest specimen she could find and then drop it through an open vent. For sailors intent on keeping our boat free from roaches, this was the worst thing and we did all we could to discourage her. She switched to shoreside rats, which was no better, and still we battled to keep the yacht vermin-free. One night a rat was dropped into the bilges and Michael leapt from his bed, grabbed a shoe and started off in hot pursuit in a bid to catch the rodent. Frightened it was going to get trapped below decks, it quickly shot outside on to the foredeck where Michael finally despatched it. It was only as fellow yachties on neighbouring craft began to cheer that he realised he had forgotten to put clothes on before giving chase.

When cruising between the islands, we would lay out astern a long line and fishing lure to trawl for our supper. Dorado or tuna were our favourites and Spinny loved her fish fresh from the sea too. As soon as the alarm went on the reel she would appear on deck, attentively watching as we wound in the long line. But sometimes, before we were halfway through reeling in and had no idea what we had caught, Spinny would walk off with a disgusted flick of her tail. We knew then we had caught a barracuda. Spinny's hatred for the shark-like fish was about more than flavour; it stemmed from the occasion when, having caught one and not knowing what to do with it, we flung it into the galley sink to be dealt with when we made harbour. It lay there apparently dormant until Spinny gave it a poke with her paw. There was a terrified shriek of cat calling and a bushy-tailed Burmese cat shot quickly up on to the deck seeking our protection when the nasty critter snapped its evil teeth-laden jaws in her direction. She would never go near another barracuda.

And then, one day, we had been attending a charter yacht show in Antigua and were just minutes from casting off and setting sail when we noticed Spinny was not in her usual sea-going comfy spot. She had been AWOL before, but she never went far and always came when we called. Sailing was delayed and we spent hours ashore looking for her.

She could not be found and so reluctantly we faced the only conclusion we could and admitted she must have run away. The dockmaster would not let us stay any longer. Despondently we rolled up the yacht's water hose, then prepared to cast off the mooring ropes and leave the dock to anchor offshore so we could continue our search ashore. As we got ready to set sail without her, Michael opened the lazarette, the large garage-like space at the yacht's stern in which we stowed fenders and awnings. Disdainfully, Spinny climbed out of the locker and rather indignantly shook her back leg at Michael – the Burmese cat equivalent of giving him the finger.

Frances Howorth is an award-winning photographer and travel writer whose specialist subject is yachts and yachting. A former council member of the British Guild of Travel Writers, she holds Yachtmaster qualifications and  writes about the lavish life at sea while photographing luxury yachts and the destinations they cruise to.

Dapple the Reluctant Donkey

John Harrison

Elaine couldn't carry her pack fifty miles over Andean passes above fifteen thousand feet. We needed a pack animal, and I would name it 'Dapple' after the beloved ass on which Sancho Panza followed Don Quixote.

We walked the countryside around the sad, dusty town of Huari following detailed directions to donkey owners only to find they were out, the donkey had been sold, there never had been a donkey, or the donkey was a horse. By day four, I would have settled for a sheep with a sound work ethic. I finally insinuated myself on to the breakfast show of the local station, Radio Colcas, run from the bedsit of Ramírez Villacorta, and explained to an extended audience of three outlying villages the donkey-shaped hole in our lives. By early next afternoon I had bought a female donkey from a man named Jesús for 550 soles.

She came with a ten-foot-long, four-inch-wide woven woollen strap with an iron ring at one end, and a yard of home-tanned leather belt, as flexible as a lobster, also with a ring at one end. With these, we were to attach to Dapple our backpacks. As we bought fodder in the market there was an endless supply of free advice on how to load Dapple, all different.

I asked, 'Which of you actually owns a donkey?' They fell silent.

The parting words of the market's butcher were, 'Keep a close watch on her for the first week, they try to come home.'

'Great,' said Elaine, 'a homing donkey.'

The packs didn't fall off for two hundred yards, which was just after we had left town. Honour was preserved.

The first aspect of Dapple's psychology which I discovered for myself was that the slightest change in my stride caused her to stop as if turned to stone. My beginning a fresh stride did not encourage her to move.

'There's something I forgot to ask.'

Elaine stopped, Dapple stopped. 'Something important?'

'Does Dapple understand Spanish, or just Quechua?'

'I don't think she understands movement.'

'You wouldn't expect them to sell us their best donkey, would you?' Even as I said it, I pictured Jesús running up the road waving 550 soles in the air, yelling, 'I can't believe they bought her.'

We tied Dapple securely to a small acacia and sat on the hedgerow bank to eat. The sound of crashing branches drew our heads round to watch her attempting to climb the tree.

We were following the floor of a narrow canyon where the light faded early, looking for a place to pitch the tent, when a tall Hispanic-looking man appeared in front of us, his face as open as a child's. I explained our walk, and without a word Juan led us into his yard where his wife Senya stood waiting, greeting two strangers as if the day had gone slowly waiting for us to arrive. 'Welcome and God bless you.' They cleared a dry shed for us to sleep in, and I tethered Dapple in their small orchard, with strict orders against further climbing.

At first light, I checked Dapple. Her rope was wrapped round her neck, all her legs, and the tree. She looked like a failed game of bondage. When I leaned on her shoulder to free her, my hand came away wet with unclotted blood that streamed down to the top of her leg. Oddly, there was no nail or wire on the tree, and when I bathed her coat I could find no wound. Juan appeared at the pump.

'Do you have vampire bats?'

'Yes! They attack livestock, and carry rabies.'

'That's all I need, a rabid homing donkey.'

Juan insisted on tying one bag across Dapple's shoulders and the other along her spine. I looked at him. 'It's fine!' he said confidently, slapping the bag on her shoulders, which slipped a foot to one side. The temperature was already eighty degrees Fahrenheit and, as we began climbing the soaring hairpins, there was no movement in the sultry air. After twenty minutes Dapple's pack again slipped to one side. I heaved it back and took up the slack in the cinch. Elaine was walking very slowly, but I knew from her breathing and pale mauve face that it wasn't through lack of effort. She placed a wad of coca leaves in her cheek and gagged. 'I'd forgotten how horrible they taste.' She took a swig of water, then dipped her finger in the white powder which helps release the active alkaloid.

Dapple wouldn't keep pace. If I had been carrying my pack myself, I would have been walking faster. The hairpins went on for an hour and a half, until, turning a flank in the hill, there was nothing in front of us but empty air. A massive landslip higher up had carried away the trail. Elaine, now a rather pleasant plum colour, walked higher up the slope. 'There's a trail made since the landslide.'

We were soon on this much narrower new path, with barely room to place my boots side by side. A glance down brought a single thought: 'One slip and I'll bounce for a thousand feet.' In the middle of a particularly narrow section, Dapple's pack slipped loose. I desperately wanted to continue to a safer place, but if the bags fell off getting there, we would never get them back. We did our first unaided loading of the donkey in the most dangerous position we would ever do it.

Elaine suggested, 'Let's lash the bags together on the ground, then hang one either side of Dapple and secure them with the cinch.' As we lifted them Dapple interpreted something I said in English as 'Giddy-up!' in Quechua, and walked away. I hopped along at her side, trying to hold on to all our luggage with one hand, and bend down to catch her lead rope with the other.

There were interludes of great pleasure. One morning took us, warm with coca-leaf tea, across haunting limestone scenery. It was glorious walking over springy turf, the trail visible across the hills far ahead. Each exposed rock, its fissures bright with the delicate orange flowers of *huamapenka*, seemed to bear the chisel marks of its own construction, but they were the solution runnels made by trickling rain, century by century. A small stream fell in miniature waterfalls to pools of white boulders. We stripped off and washed from head to toe, taking turns, since there was nowhere to tie Dapple. Two naked white people chasing a donkey across a plain could change the myths of a generation. Dapple's contribution to the toiletries was to stand upstream and piss, sending me scuttling until the yellow slick had passed.

I said, 'Did you see how she did that?'

'Are there two ways to pee?'

'*She* used a large grey penis: we have a castrated male. Perhaps that accounts for its great suspicion of humans.'

Elaine bent down, 'You're right.'

'Men know about these things.'

I became more sympathetic. Dapple did not. The final section of the fifty miles was a magnificent Inca stair as fine as any we had seen. The sweeping turns down the face of the hillside were breathtakingly assured. At the foot it spilled us on to the riverbank where a log bridge passed high over the waters, and we headed across the fields to the road. There was no breeze in the valley floor and in early afternoon it was stiflingly hot. Elaine said, 'I'll take Dapple now we're on the flat, give you a break.'

Dapple, who might, in his goldfish memory, have forgotten what traffic was, became hysterical. He would not walk along the road unless led on a short rope and poked on the backside with a stick every three yards. Every fifty yards he tried to run over the road, stampede into a field or yard, or jump down into the ditch. When heading the right way he crawled, or just stopped. All diversions were done at speeds ranging up to full gallop. A great criminal mind could not have plotted more effectively to ruin the walk. Soon Elaine was at her wits' end, pulled about the road. After a particularly purple outburst I took Dapple back. Within three minutes I was coming out with worse. Dapple had now shaken the bags loose. Those four miles on a level road, by a beautiful river, were some of the longest and most miserable on the whole trip.

When travel writers, particularly British ones, work with unfamiliar animals, it is customary to record a period of initial difficulties, where it seems as if the animal will never be tractable. This is followed by useful tips from locals and a realisation that one's own ignorance was causing many of the difficulties. Eventually the animal will, at a point where the success of the venture hangs in the balance, perform some act of magnificent endurance or courage; all is forgiven, and, at the end of the trip, there is a tearful parting, at least on the side of the human, and, as for the animal – well, if only they could speak.

I want to say that I shall hate that little bastard until the end of time.

If you feel yourself incapable of violence towards animals, which I do, there are few better ways to test it than by working with a donkey which is carrying everything you need in the world to keep you alive, and only manages a speed faster than that of vegetables growing when it has slipped round behind you, and begun to gallop back down a hill which it has taken you five hours to climb. Should you catch it up, you will find yourself eyeball to eyeball, trembling with fury, describing with great relish and an almost sexual gratification, exactly how, if it does not contribute a little more to the expedition's aims and ambitions, you are going to kill it, cook it and eat it. Vivisection, you will tell it, is too good for it.

In between, when it makes a slight effort to move your luggage in the direction you wish to go, at one-third the pace you could carry the donkey and the luggage yourself, you will fawn on him, pat the soft fringe coming down over his nose, whisper sweet quadruped nothings in his ear. He will smile, as nearly as he can, knowing he has won.

I ended up walking ahead of Dapple, the rope over my shoulder, dragging him along, as if I were one of the Volga boatmen. Having hoped, at one time, to be in La Union in time for a late lunch, we limped into town around five.

A year later I gave a talk about my trip to the Royal Geographical Society. When I showed a slide of Dapple, his hair falling coyly over his eyes, hiding the malice, and his body language that of Eeyore on receipt of a telegram cancelling Christmas, an uncharacteristically soft noise fluttered round the Ondaatje Theatre. It was the sound of cooing underpinned by *aaahs* of misplaced sympathy. I had to stop them siding with the enemy. I flourished a news clipping: 'This is from *The Times* of 21st May 2013. "Magyarszecsod: A Hungarian man died after being dragged off his mobility scooter, trampled on and bitten. Sandor Horvath, sixty-five, was attacked at a farm while visiting a friend. It was thought that he had been attacked by wild dogs but the bites proved to be from donkeys.'"

The audience did not believe a word of it.

John Harrison's journeys have taken him from Greenland to Antarctica via the jungles of Central America and the mountains of Peru. Accolades for his books include the Wales Book of the Year. In *1519: A Journey to the End of Time,* he describes his efforts to die in the footsteps of Hernán Cortés. For more see: www.cloudroad.co.uk.

EUROPE

Goldfish Trek

Emma Macdonald

I remember feeling like a sheriff when I put my prefect's badge on to the headmaster's desk, handing in my notice. When he asked me if I wanted to think about it I said I already had. My school was so surprised, they banned my goldfish. I had no regrets, but the kitchen staff were sad for me. 'She has to give her goldfish away!' Dorothy said, and the others started tut-tutting.

The perk of being able to keep a pet at my English boarding school in the late 1970s was for prefects only. Other girls had horses, guinea pigs and rabbits – and I had picked a fish. I had cleaned the fishbowl every few weeks, done everything the pet shop told me to do after finally selecting a pretty orange fantail goldfish from all the others in a tank, the assistant chasing carefully around with a net until I said, 'Yes, that one!'

Back at school I found a safe place for it on my chest of drawers away from direct sunlight, as advised. I prepared the spherical fishbowl I bought with little stones and real weed the fish could eat to supplement the fish food. Then I made sure the fish stayed in its bag while half filling the fishbowl, waiting for the temperatures of both to equalise, using cold water from the bathroom tap, before emptying the fish into the bowl. From then on I fed him every day and changed his water every two weeks.

While having George was considered a privilege and I enjoyed looking after him, it was some of my prefect duties I found tiresome, one being to ring the bells on the hour every Saturday morning so that classes could start and stop. Occasionally I would forget because I was reading a good novel or making coffee or gossiping. Also I didn't have a watch. A deeper reason for feeling uncomfortable with the role was my sensing that I was only really made a prefect to be a diplomat among the foreign girls because I was born in Switzerland to English parents and bilingual, so they couldn't decide whether I was English or foreign.

But the main reason I 'resigned' was Leslie, who had stood by my grandmother when my grandfather died when I was six.

They had been close ever since, despite never marrying, and he had become a member of my family, despite my mother disliking him. Leslie was a very sweet and amusing man, and while my mother tried to prevent us from liking him she didn't succeed. When I was eleven he would visit us from England, and in the fields and woods find fireflies in the evenings. He'd tell me how he used to go scrumping apples when he was my age and told me always to have a piece of string, a penknife and a safety pin in my pocket. He once used the penknife to cut some mistletoe from a tree.

I had been at my boarding school for about a year and was aged about sixteen when I received a call from my grandmother one day to say that Leslie had died. 'Oh Nana,' I said, and stood silently, feeling completely cold. She explained that he had died while they were on holiday together. 'I'll try to come and see you,' I said.

When I told the headmaster about it and asked if I could go to my grandmother he refused, saying that Leslie wasn't related to me. My parents didn't go to Leslie's funeral either and my father cracked a joke about him probably dying from shock at the bill at the hotel they were at when it happened. There was no point explaining to any of them that I loved Leslie. A month later my mother flew in to visit my grandmother and I asked if I could join them. The headmaster said no, and I said, 'Well I'm leaving the school.'

Taking the goldfish in its bowl and my bag, I left everything else of mine behind and rang a taxi, deciding that my grandmother would get my fish. I went down as I saw it pull up in the courtyard and my housemistress came running up behind me, out of breath, saying, 'The headmaster said you can go!' 'I was going in any case,' I replied, running down the stairs, careful not to let any water spill. The trouble was I hadn't really worked out the logistics of getting a goldfish in a bowl full of water, stones and weed from a school in rural Hertfordshire to my grandmother in Kent by train to King's Cross, taxi to Charing Cross and train to Bexleyheath with all the stops and starts in between.

Other girls came with me in the taxi and we took turns holding George as we unrolled our forbidden jeans we'd hidden under our skirts. George swam happily as his water sloshed around, his bowl topped with cling film, which soon became wet and stopped clinging, and water spilt whenever I yanked my bag on to my shoulder. 'Mind you keep water off the seats!' said the driver. 'Mind you keep your eyes on the road!' snapped Vicky.

'Fish got a ticket, has he?' asked the stationmaster.

Eventually I hooked my bag over my head so it wouldn't keep slipping off. On the train a man offered to hold the bowl while I put my bag on the luggage rack. At King's Cross I topped up George's water and found a taxi queue. 'Sorry, no pets,' one said, so I went searching for the Underground. Struggling to prop the bowl against the ticket office window, I fumbled for my purse as another man held the bowl. At the ticket barrier, now rush hour, I balanced it again.

As there were no seats on the Tube, I stood with George under my arm and water splashed out whenever people jostled on and off. Some landed on a man's newspaper which he flicked huffily.

Finally at Bexleyheath, hours later, the fishbowl was in a telephone box balanced on a row of phone books. I remembered how Leslie would usually wait here patiently to pick me up, talking to the guards. It was getting dark and I walked the last mile or so to my grandmother's house, just managing to reach the doorbell.

'I have a fish for you.' I mentioned nothing about my badge, foreign girls not being made prefects, refused visits, my housemistress chasing me, or my parents not exactly helping. They were trivialities compared with my grandmother's feelings for Leslie.

'What a dear little thing! He'll be someone to talk to,' she replied, taking the bowl.

'It might need a bit more water,' I said. And that evening as we watched TV, George watched it too from his bowl.

Emma Macdonald is a freelance writer and artist. Born in Switzerland, she went to school in Switzerland, France and England and lived in Tasmania where she brought up her five children with  her husband John, wrote features for Australian newspapers and designed greeting cards. She moved to England in 2009.

From *Travels with a Donkey in the Cévennes*

Robert Louis Stevenson

It was 1878 and Robert Louis Stevenson was in his late twenties when he spent a month in Le Monastier, near Le Puy, preparing for a journey south through the Cévennes in south-central France. The villagers, unused to seeing such travellers, were eager to be involved in his preparations. 'I was looked upon with contempt, like a man who should project a journey to the moon, but yet with a respectful interest, like one setting forth for the inclement Pole.'

It remained to choose a beast of burden. Now, a horse is a fine lady among animals, flighty, timid, delicate in eating, of tender health; he is too valuable and too restive to be left alone, so that you are chained to your brute as to a fellow galley-slave; a dangerous road puts him out of his wits; in short, he's an uncertain and exacting ally, and adds thirty-fold to the troubles of the voyager. What I required was something cheap and small and hardy, and of a stolid and peaceful temper; and all these requisites pointed to a donkey.

There dwelt an old man in Monastier, of rather unsound intellect according to some, much followed by street boys, and known to fame as Father Adam. Father Adam had a cart, and to draw the cart a diminutive she-ass, not much bigger than a dog, the colour of a mouse, with a kindly eye and a determined under-jaw. There was something neat and highbred, a Quakerish elegance, about the rogue that hit my fancy on the spot. Our first interview was in Monastier marketplace. To prove her good temper, one child after another was set upon her back to ride, and one after another went head over heels into the air; until a want of confidence began to reign in youthful bosoms, and the experiment was discontinued from a dearth of subjects. I was already backed by a deputation of my friends; but as if this were not enough, all the buyers and sellers came round and helped me in the bargain; and the ass and I and Father Adam were the centre of a hubbub for near half an hour. At length she passed into my service for the consideration of sixty-five francs and a glass of brandy. The sack had already cost eighty francs and two glasses of beer; so that 'Modestine', as I instantly baptised her, was upon all accounts the cheaper article. Indeed, that was as it should be; for she was only an appurtenance of my mattress, or self-acting bedstead on four castors.

I had a last interview with Father Adam in a billiard room at the witching hour of dawn, when I administered the brandy. He professed himself greatly touched by the separation, and declared he had often bought white bread for the donkey when he had been content with black bread for himself; but this, according to the best authorities, must have been a flight of fancy. He had a name in the village for brutally misusing the ass; yet it is certain that he shed a tear, and the tear made a clean mark down one cheek.

By the advice of a fallacious local saddler, a leather pad was made for me with rings to fasten on my bundle; and I thoughtfully completed my kit and arranged my toilette. By way of armoury and utensils, I took a revolver, a little spirit lamp and pan, a lantern and some halfpenny candles, a jack-knife and a large leather flask. The main cargo consisted of two entire changes of warm clothing – besides my travelling wear of country velveteen, pilot-coat and knitted spencer – some books and my railway rug, which, being also in the form of a bag, made me a double castle for cold nights. The permanent larder was represented by cakes of chocolate and tins of Bologna sausage. All this, except what I carried about my person, was easily stowed into the sheepskin bag; and by good fortune I threw in my empty knapsack, rather for convenience of carriage than from any thought that I should want it on my journey. For more immediate needs I took a leg of cold mutton, a bottle of Beaujolais, an empty bottle to carry milk, an egg-beater and a considerable quantity of black bread and white, like Father Adam, for myself and donkey, only in my scheme of things the destinations were reversed.

On the day of my departure I was up a little after five; by six, we began to load the donkey; and ten minutes after, my hopes were in the dust. The pad would not stay on Modestine's back for half a moment. I returned it to its maker, with whom I had so contumelious a passage that the street outside was crowded from wall to wall with gossips looking on and listening. The pad changed hands with much vivacity; perhaps it would be more descriptive to say that we threw it at each other's heads; and, at any rate, we were very warm and unfriendly, and spoke with a deal of freedom.

I had a common donkey packsaddle – a *barde*, as they call it – fitted upon Modestine; and once more loaded her with my effects. The doubled sack, my pilot-coat (for it was warm, and I was to walk in my waistcoat), a great bar of black bread and an open basket containing the white bread, the mutton and the bottles, were all corded together in a very elaborate system of knots, and I looked on the result with fatuous content. In such a monstrous deck-cargo, all poised above the donkey's shoulders, with nothing below to balance, on a brand-new packsaddle that had not yet been worn to fit the animal, and fastened with brand-new girths that might be expected to stretch and slacken by the way, even a very careless traveller should have seen disaster brewing. That elaborate system of knots, again, was the work of too many sympathisers to be very artfully designed. It is true they tightened the cords with a will; as many as three at a time would have a foot against Modestine's quarters, and be hauling with clenched teeth; but I learned afterwards that one thoughtful person, without any exercise of force, can make a more solid job than half a dozen heated and enthusiastic grooms. I was then but a novice; even after the misadventure of the pad nothing could disturb my security, and I went forth from the stable door as an ox goeth to the slaughter.

The Green Donkey Driver

The bell of Monastier was just striking nine as I got quit of these preliminary troubles and descended the hill through the common. As long as I was within sight of the windows, a secret shame and the fear of some laughable defeat withheld me from tampering with Modestine. She tripped along upon her four small hoofs with a sober daintiness of gait; from time to time she shook her ears or her tail; and she looked so small under the bundle that my mind misgave me. We got across the ford without difficulty – there was no doubt about the matter, she was docility itself – and once on the other bank, where the road begins to mount through pinewoods, I took in my right hand the unhallowed staff, and with a quaking spirit applied it to the donkey. Modestine brisked up her pace for perhaps three steps, and then relapsed into her former minuet. Another application had the same effect, and so with the third. I am worthy the name of an Englishman, and it goes against my conscience to lay my hand rudely on a female. I desisted, and looked her all over from head to foot; the poor brute's knees were trembling and her breathing was distressed; it was plain that she could go no faster on a hill. God forbid, thought I, that I should brutalise this innocent creature; let her go at her own pace, and let me patiently follow.

What that pace was, there is no word mean enough to describe; it was something as much slower than a walk as a walk is slower than a run; it kept me hanging on each foot for an incredible length of time; in five minutes it exhausted the spirit and set up a fever in all the muscles of the leg. And yet I had to keep close at hand and measure my advance exactly upon hers; for if I dropped a few yards into the rear, or went on a few yards ahead, Modestine came instantly to a halt and began to browse. The thought that this was to last from here to Alais nearly broke my heart. Of all conceivable journeys, this promised to be the most tedious. I tried to tell myself it was a lovely day; I tried to charm my foreboding spirit with tobacco; but I had a vision ever present to me of the long, long roads, up hill and down dale, and a pair of figures ever infinitesimally moving, foot by foot, a yard to the minute, and, like things enchanted in a nightmare, approaching no nearer to the goal.

In the meantime there came up behind us a tall peasant, perhaps forty years of age, of an ironical snuffy countenance, and arrayed in the green tailcoat of the country. He overtook us hand over hand, and stopped to consider our pitiful advance.

'Your donkey,' says he, 'is very old?'

I told him, I believed not.

Then, he supposed, we had come far.

I told him, we had but newly left Monastier.

'*Et vous marchez comme ça!*' cried he; and, throwing back his head, he laughed long and heartily. I watched him, half-prepared to feel offended, until he had satisfied his mirth; and then, 'You must have no pity on these animals,' said he; and, plucking a switch out of a thicket, he began to lace Modestine about the stern-works, uttering a cry. The rogue pricked up her ears and broke into a good round pace, which she kept up without flagging, and without exhibiting the least symptom of distress, as long as the peasant kept beside us. Her former panting and shaking had been, I regret to say, a piece of comedy.

It was blazing hot up the valley, windless, with vehement sun upon my shoulders; and I had to labour so consistently with my stick that the sweat ran into my eyes. Every five minutes, too, the pack, the basket and the pilot-coat would take an ugly slew to one side or the other; and I had to stop Modestine, just when I had got her to a tolerable pace of about two miles an hour, to tug, push, shoulder and readjust the load. And at last, in the village of Ussel, saddle and all, the whole hypothec turned round and grovelled in the dust below the donkey's belly. She, none better pleased, incontinently drew up and seemed to smile; and a party of one man, two women and two children came up, and, standing round me in a half-circle, encouraged her by their example.

I had the devil's own trouble to get the thing righted; and the instant I had done so, without hesitation, it toppled and fell down upon the other side. Judge if I was hot! And yet not a hand was offered to assist me. The man, indeed, told me I ought to have a package of a different shape. I suggested, if he knew nothing better to the point in my predicament, he might hold his tongue. And the good-natured dog agreed with me smilingly. It was the most despicable fix. I must plainly content myself with the pack for Modestine, and take the following items for my own share of the portage: a cane, a quart-flask, a pilot-jacket heavily weighted in the pockets, two pounds of black bread and an open basket full of meats and bottles. I believe I may say I am not devoid of greatness of soul; for I did not recoil from this infamous burden. I disposed it, Heaven knows how, so as to be mildly portable, and then proceeded to steer Modestine through the village. She tried, as was indeed her invariable habit, to enter every house and every courtyard in the whole length; and, encumbered as I was, without a hand to help myself, no words can render an idea of my difficulties. A priest, with six or seven others, was examining a church in process of repair, and he and his acolytes laughed loudly as they saw my plight.

I remembered having laughed myself when I had seen good men struggling with adversity in the person of a jackass, and the recollection filled me with penitence.

Born in 1850 in Edinburgh, Scotland, **Robert Louis Stevenson** compulsively wrote stories throughout a childhood dogged by illness and in his early twenties was sent to France for his health, returning to travel there many times. His first travel book was about a canoe trip in Belgium and France, *An Inland Voyage* (1878), and his next was *Travels with a Donkey in the Cévennes* (1879). He later became a novelist, poet and essayist, famous for *Treasure Island*, *Kidnapped* and *Strange Case of Dr Jekyll and Mr Hyde*. He died in the Samoan Islands.

Monty in a Basket

Mike Gerrard

The journey from Belsize Park to Canvey Island may not be one of the world's greatest road trips, even if it does take you through Ilford, Dagenham and Basildon, but sharing a car with a python certainly adds a frisson to the drive.

My new girlfriend was an unlikely combination of half-Malaysian, half-Irish, and had told me at first that she was a belly dancer, though always parried my requests to come and watch her at work. Eventually she told me she had a gig at a party in east London that I could come to, but she needed a new costume and different music. She lived in Belsize Park in one of several flats above an Asian mini-market, and we wandered backstreets buying material from Indian clothes shops, and spent a happy afternoon sewing sequins on her bra. I could sew a button on a shirt, but putting sequins on a bra was more of a challenge.

We set off to somewhere east of Aldgate. In a huge, private hired room, an East End knees-up was going on, to celebrate someone's wedding anniversary. Simone, as I'll call her, was the entertainment. I watched from the bar as she went through her paces, slightly worried that her sequins might fall off. As she finished her act with a swirl of red and gold silk scarves, I followed her into the dressing room, where she was glistening with sweat.

'I've got a confession to make,' she said.

'What's that?'

'I've never done a belly dance before in my life.'

I couldn't believe it. She'd made the whole thing up as she went along: the hip shaking, the belly rolling, the hand movements, everything.

'That's why I needed a new outfit and new music. I've never done it before.'

Shortly after, Simone invited me along to see her perform at a pub in Canvey Island one Sunday. It seemed an odd venue for a belly dance, but what did I know? I'd never been to this brash Essex seaside resort before. We drove past fairground rides, arcades of gaming machines with optimistic names like Las Vegas, and ended up in a pub that was jam-packed with Sunday lunchtime drinkers having a loud good time. In the dressing room Simone put on her costume, sequins still securely in place, and asked me to watch her from the bar and let her know what I thought of her performance.

I got a pint and joined the rest of the men in the pub, who went silent when the music started, all eyes turned to the stage. Simone danced out from the dressing room, swirling her red-and-gold scarves around and twisting her arms, just as I'd seen her do before. I was so naive that I wasn't expecting what happened next, as Simone slowly and suggestively took her bra off. It dawned on me that my new girlfriend was a stripper, a fact confirmed when the rest of her outfit came off too.

She told me later that she'd been a stripper for a few years, but never told her boyfriends that until she got to know them better. She was worried that they would prejudge her, assuming that all strippers were slappers. I understood totally. I might have done the same, but now that I'd got to know her, I liked the person she was. The fact that she was a stripper was definitely a surprise, but it didn't change who she was in my eyes.

And then Monty Python entered the picture.

I'd started going with Simone to as many of her gigs as I could manage, both to enjoy her company and to be the minder/boyfriend, keeping unwanted attention away. I'd met lots of other strippers, and their partners. One dancer was married to a lawyer, another was a teacher who only danced at weekends, and never anywhere close to where she lived. All the girls had a stage name and a real name, and only friends knew their real names. In the pubs and clubs and to their agents, they always used their stage name, separating the work from themselves.

Like all self-employed people, they took what work came their way, as Simone had done when her agent asked her if she could do the belly dancing gig as he didn't have a belly dancer on his books. Simone's dusky Malaysian looks made her fit the bill.

So when she was offered another booking as a snake dancer, she said yes and then worried about finding a snake. She asked one of her stripper friends, a tall blonde called Barbara, who was happy to loan her python named Monty to Simone. Monty was a little lethargic, as Barbara had been cooling him down, which made him more docile and easier to transport.

'About half an hour before you go on,' she told us, 'you need to warm him up a little so he'll wake up. You need to put some hot water in his hot-water bottle. Here it is.'

I found myself holding Monty's hot-water bottle, which was slightly bizarre but not as bizarre as what came next. Pythons aren't poisonous, but they can still bite. They're not serious bites, more like a pinprick, and while the owner might know this, you didn't really want Monty sinking his teeth into an audience member who startled it.

To avoid such a possibility, Barbara showed us how she put tape around Monty's jaws so that he couldn't open them, but could still flick his tongue out and look suitably menacing and snakelike.

'He's quite used to it, and it doesn't hurt him at all. You can leave it on till you bring him back. The tape can shine a bit in the spotlight, so you need to camouflage it so no-one can see it,' Barbara instructed.

And so it was that I found myself painting mascara on the Sellotape, matching the patterns on Monty's green-and-black skin.

Barbara slid Monty into his basket, a round rattan affair with, I was pleased to see, a top on it. I was put in charge of Monty for the night, and carried him down to the car for the drive out to Canvey Island, an exotic destination I was becoming familiar with. Not to a pub this time, but to a holiday camp, where Simone would be keeping her clothes on. It was surprising how one outfit could serve for belly dancing, stripping and now snake dancing.

We put Monty on the back seat, and I sat the whole journey leaning round with my hand firmly on top of the basket. Monty might be docile, but I'd never been that close to a snake before, and the thought of carrying him in my lap made me nervous. I can't imagine why.

We found the holiday camp dancehall where Simone was to do her stuff. There was a stage at one end and the dance floor was covered with tables where couples, families, friends, young and old, all sat round enjoying their drinks and chicken-in-a-basket. Little did they know what I had in my basket as I carried Monty into the dressing room behind the stage, though the few people who spotted us were obviously intrigued.

I found my way to the kitchen and asked if they could boil me a kettle of hot water.

'I can make you a pot of tea, love, you don't have to make it yourself.'

'No, it's just the hot water I need.'

'Are you not feeling well?'

I explained I needed the water to warm up the snake for the act. They boiled me a kettle and I got more curious looks as I carried it back to the dressing room, where I poured it into Monty's hot-water bottle. Then came the moment of truth. We had to put the hot-water bottle into the basket, underneath Monty. We peered in. He looked quite harmless, lying quietly there.

'You lift him out,' I said, 'and I'll put the bottle in.'

'No, you lift him out.'

'You're going to be dancing with him, you ought to get to know him.'

I got the look. I lifted Monty out and Simone put the bottle in. He was definitely docile, but awake. His body was warm and surprisingly dry. His tongue flicked out as he sensed the air around him. I could feel the strength in the body, and would not like to get on the wrong side of Monty. I put him back in his basket and we planned the show.

Simone would start with a bit of exotic dancing, which basically meant waving her arms around and swirling her scarves again. She would make her way to the far end of the room, and while people were hopefully looking that way, I would sneak on to the stage and deposit Monty's basket in the middle. This was showbiz! People would turn round in their seats as Simone danced back on to the stage.

From the dressing room I could hear the murmurs from the audience and could tell they were curious. I watched from the wings as Simone stood and swayed behind the basket and lifted the top off with a theatrical flourish. She reached inside and lifted Monty out, holding him by what would have been his neck if a snake had a neck, and by roughly where his hips would have been.

Monty was definitely warming up, and wriggling slightly, though it looked more like someone stretching than anything dangerous. He wrapped his tail around Simone's wrist and behaved suitably snakelike,

like the old pro he was. Monty was definitely a hit. Some people screamed as Simone approached, causing everyone else to laugh, until it was their turn to get up close. Monty writhed as sensuously as Simone did, while she worked the room and made sure every table got a look – and a touch if they wanted. She draped Monty around the necks of a few of the braver souls, and pretended to chase children who went squealing from the room.

Eventually, timing it to the pace of the music, she returned to the stage and put Monty back into his basket, and closed the lid. The music ended and she bowed to a huge round of applause and whistles.

We ate our own post-show chickens-in-a-basket, and then drove Monty back home, my hand still firmly on the top of his basket, though by now I was brave enough to hold it in my lap. I needed a firm grip as Monty was still frisky, and the basket would occasionally lurch as he moved around, though as he got colder he wriggled less and less. We delivered him safely back to Barbara, to the great relief of everyone – especially me. It might not be Route 66, but the A13 to Canvey Island certainly has its kicks when you drive it with a snake and a stripper.

Mike Gerrard is an award-winning travel and drinks writer, contributing to publications worldwide. He's written over forty guidebooks, one podcast, three radio plays, a collection of travel writing entitled  *Snakes Alive* and a crime novel, *Strip Till Dead*. He splits his time between Cambridgeshire and Arizona.

Smuggling Fleur

Hugh Tucker

Smuggling, as a crime that has existed ever since men created borders, has somehow managed to struggle through the ages with its nose reasonably clean, at least as far as its public image is concerned. This has been helped along by the unscrupulously romantic writings of Daphne du Maurier, Faulkner and Hemingway, and TV dramas featuring a rugged and windswept Cornish coastline and equally rugged and windswept protagonists. It's far more Han Solo than Hannibal Lecter as far as common perception goes, and, in retrospect, it was perhaps this rather misplaced affection for this particular brand of criminality that made the whole thing seem so exciting.

I was twelve years old and staying with my family in a rented cottage in the northwest of France, not so far from Mont-Saint-Michel. Holidays at this age were mostly a blur of excitement; so involved was I in the feast of new experiences and different places that I failed to pause and commit much of them to memory. But this particular holiday was a little different. So striking was the effect of my new-found companion that I remember the patchwork of cinnamon and faded green fields that stretched out forever in all directions; the sharp crack of French bangers that consumed most of my pocket money; the strange painting of a clown that hung in my sister's bedroom and gave her nightmares. Most of all, I remember Fleur.

Fleur, though not yet bearing that name, came to our attention during the first few days of our stay. Buzzards are not particularly discreet, and her mother's wailing call and elegant, wheeling glide soon betrayed her nest, which was nestled in a crevice in the wall, just beneath my bedroom window.

Pleasant days passed, punctuated by the cries of our resident bird of prey and meals on the terrace watching her bring her own, rather less appetising, dinner back to her young. The buzzards merged into the ambience of the countryside, merely one more picturesque piece of the puzzle. To tell the truth I thought very little about them, that is until I found Fleur in a flowerbed whilst extricating a tennis ball.

I could easily have overlooked her, had it not been for the extent to which the ball had become lodged in the thick undergrowth. Tangled in an unfamiliar nest at ground level was a miserable little creature that seemed to be more fluff than feathers.

At first, I didn't know what to do. I thought perhaps her mother might yet find her and I remembered distinctly that if a human touched a wild chick, it would be shunned by its natural parents. But upon running to tell my father, and after he had come to look at the hapless thing, he explained that her wing was broken and she wouldn't survive if we left her there.

He fetched a tea towel from the kitchen and, carefully pushing aside the plants, swaddled Fleur and carried her into the kitchen, where we set about making an improvised nest out of a biscuit tin and cotton wool. As comfortable as we tried to make her, poor Fleur was terrified; her little body trembled and shook to such a degree that I was afraid she would perish then and there. It was then that she was given her name, as my mother picked off the petals of a flower that were stuck to her body.

The holiday changed somewhat at this point. The carefree days were replaced by hours of emotional investment watching over the chick and willing her to get stronger. My parents had to constantly remind my sister and me not to fuss over her and to give her some peace. Trips into the nearby village were now marked by a visit to the *boucherie*, where my parents' broken French and descriptions of a '*grand oiseau*' resulted in a plastic bag of finely diced steak. We fed her and gave her water using the tip of a feather. She began to grow stronger and started to seem more comfortable – she was certainly more vocal – and we could hardly contain our delight as it looked certain that she would fully recover.

But holidays must end, and ours was no exception. As I sat down to our final dinner, Fleur's tin occupying pride of place at the head of the table, I raised the question of where Fleur was going to sit in the car. My mother caught my father's eye. I had unwittingly triggered a discussion that I'm sure my father had hoped to avoid. My mother told me that we couldn't bring her back, as not only was it not allowed, but it also wouldn't be good for her. We were going to ask the owner of the chateau to take her to a vet and send us the bill. My father remained silent, but he caught my eye and very subtly mouthed, 'I'll speak to her.'

The next morning, after rising early to pack, the situation of Fleur had obviously been settled, as placed on the middle seat in the back of the car was a large cardboard box that had been perforated to allow air in, inside of which was Fleur's tin. My dad gave me a little wink in the rear-view mirror.

The journey to Calais was remarkably straightforward. I left the top of the box open to give Fleur light and air, and apart from the occasional panic, where she would bleat and flap her good wing, she kept very quiet.

It was when we reached the ferry terminal that things changed slightly. We had been driving for a little over two hours and Fleur was beginning to resent her cardboard confines. We had joined the queue of cars boarding and my father told me to put a blanket on top of the box. As we were about to drive on to the loading ramp, the head of an official appeared through the driver's side window, but after a cursory glance he waved us on through. We breathed a sigh of relief. After we parked, I accompanied my father as he bought a well-deserved cup of tea.

In my mind we were home free, and as the ferry approached the white cliffs, we sat in the car and I opened the box up to see how Fleur was doing. The car started and we were trundling off and back on to terra firma. We were stopped again. This time a customs officer demanded, 'Do you have anything to declare?' I prayed silently that Fleur would stay still and joined my family's innocent chorus of 'No, nothing.' He seemed to stand in silence for an age. I was sure that at any moment Fleur would move or cry out.

But after a short eternity, he nodded and waved us on. The relief was immense and Fleur seemed to be able to sense that something had happened as she joined the excited chatter. We were now all successful smugglers, or at least accomplices, and I must say it felt good.

Hugh Tucker has been writing articles about travel and works of fiction since leaving university. He lives in London and has previously lived and worked in South Africa, where he shared his apartment with a green mamba. You can read more at: www.thetinboat.wordpress.com.

From *High Albania*

Edith Durham
Selected and introduced by Elizabeth Gowing

From 1900 to 1914, British traveller Edith Durham explored the Balkans extensively on horseback. Initially her journeys were a form of therapy following what we would probably now call a nervous breakdown and the advice of her doctor to travel. But soon she became an authority on the region, writing seven books, and was eventually appointed vice president of the Royal Anthropological Institute (the first woman to hold the position) for her studies of the places she rode to. Finding herself in countries at times of crisis she was also active in the distribution of humanitarian aid, when her horses took her to remote villages and mountain communities. In Albania and Kosovo her contribution is commemorated today in roads and schools named after her.

These extracts describing her adventures on horseback are from her best-known book, High Albania. *Her journey began in what she calls by its Italian name of Scutari, known to the Albanians as Shkodra.*

It was Friday, 8th May 1908, and Scutari was asleep – even the dogs were still curled up tight in the gutters – when we started on foot and purposely oozed out of the town by the wrong road in the grey dawning. The *kirijee* and the two horses met us in the open. It was not until we had mounted that I felt the journey had really begun at last.

There is a peculiar pleasure in riding out into the unknown – a pleasure which no second journey on the same trail ever affords.

The great mountains towered mauve in the beyond across the plain. We turned our horses off the rough track, and, following the kirijee, plunged them breast-deep into pink asphodel, hoary with dew.

From Shkodra she travelled further north, to the mountain community of Skreli where she attended the local saint's day celebrations. In attendance were the archbishop and deputy archbishop from the city of Shkodra.

There being no hay or corn, the horses of the entire party had been turned loose to browse in the copses. Consequently we awoke to a horseless dawn. The sturdy ecclesiastical steeds, not seeing the fun of fasting on a feast day, had all bolted in search of richer fare, the Archbishop's along with the rest.

My humble kirijee horses, having no superfluous energy, were found after an hour's search. Leaving the horseless churchmen disconsolate on the balcony, we started for Lower Kastrati with a Kastrati man – brother of the one who had brought us – a lively fellow, with shaven temples and hair plastered down in a straight fringe over his shaven forehead.

He had enjoyed the *festa* vastly, and fired off his whole belt of cartridges – forty. This is all that most men possess. They buy caps and powder, cast their own bullets and perpetually refill their empty cartridge cases...

We walked all down the valley of the Proni Thaat, a strip of cultivated land sown with maize and tobacco, flanked by grey, grim Karst, which nought but centuries of foresting can hope to tame. By the trackside we passed a Christian grave, adorned with a cross and a rude relief of a saddle horse. Both guide and kirijee said it was customary to carve a man's favourite horse on his grave. Does it tell of the days when a warrior's horse was buried with him?

I saw other examples.

We turned off Proni Thaat at Ura Zais, and struck over the flat plain to Baitza, past rich fields where the crops were guarded from the Evil Eye by horses' skulls set on poles, or their modern substitutes, twisted petroleum cans whitewashed.

Later her ride through the mountains took her to a bivouac at Puka where she writes evocatively of a night spent in the company of her horses and dogs.

There was a red glow of firelight and a crackling shower of sparks as dry brushwood was piled on. The picketed horses munched steadily at a feed of maize. Over all was the intense blue depths of the cloudless night sky, ablaze with a myriad stars. I wondered why people ever lived in houses as I rolled up in my rug on the hay bed.

Two faithful dogs guarded us all night, and had they not chosen my hay as the most comfortable place to sleep in, and barked loudly close to my ear whenever an imaginary danger threatened, I should have slept very well. But to lie awake under the stars is not the misery of sleeplessness in a room – rather it is pure joy. I saw them fade slowly as the dawn crept up – the crescent moon hung low – there came a dash of brilliant yellow over the hills – another day had begun.

Elizabeth Gowing is the author of *Travels in Blood and Honey; becoming a beekeeper in Kosovo*, *The Rubbish-Picker's Wife; an unlikely friendship in Kosovo* and *The Silver Thread; a journey through Balkan*  craftsmanship. Her second book, *Edith and I* focuses on Edith Durham. She divides her time between Albania, the UK and Kosovo.

Edith Durham (1863–1944) was born in London and trained as as artist at the Royal Academy of Arts. She travelled in the Balkans for two decades.

Polly Kala

Mary Johns

It was during our second summer at our Greek island home that we realised we had rats. We used to hear them pattering across the roof at night and would sit in the evening and watch them climb up the stone wall of our ancient olive-grower's cottage, as indifferent to our presence as a horse to a fly. We would, we thought, rather have cats than rats so we found two semi-wild, pretty little brown-black-and-white kittens and took them home. We called them 'Polly' and 'Kala', because *poli kala* means 'very good' in Greek.

That summer, friends were staying in our house while we were away, and we left a note asking them to feed the cats from the sack of dried food, adding in bold lettering, 'These are wild cats. Please, on no account allow them into the house.'

We got back at the beginning of September just as our guests were leaving.

Had they had a nice time? Wonderful. Was the weather good? Fantastic. What about the cats? Were they still around? Yes, up on the bed.

So there we were with two large kittens, firmly of the opinion that they belonged not in the wild but in the house, and we realised very quickly that they were so tame it would be impossible to turn them out at the end of the season. They would die. So what to do?

Off we went to the vet and he told us he could organise pet passports that would allow them into the UK. He gave them their rabies injections, lots of other injections and then microchipped them and then, at considerable expense, handed over their passports. Sorted.

Or not. At that time it wasn't possible to fly animals off the island. So when it was time to leave, instead of boarding the plane home Geoff and I took a taxi into town and began our journey from Greece to England with one suitcase and two cats in a basket.

We began by boarding the bus which would travel on the ferry from the island to Kyllini on the mainland and then for an hour or so to Patras where we would board the ferry to Venice. The cats were very quiet, obviously bemused and probably not a little frightened at the strange, swaying journey they were taking. But could we take them on the ferry? It took two nights to reach its destination. We wanted to keep them with us, but weren't sure if they would be allowed on board. We decided to smuggle them in.

With beating hearts we agreed that we would hide the cat basket in the large gym bag our friend Vivvi had sewn for us in case of just such an emergency. We would just have to hope that the steward who led us to our cabin would assume it was ordinary luggage and that the cats would not give us away.

Success! No-one noticed. We could now take the litter tray out of the suitcase, put it in the shower room and settle in.

The first day went smoothly and the kittens settled on our bunks that night as if shipboard life was for them.

Day two dawned and it was my turn to go on deck for some fresh air, but I had no sooner got up there than I realised I had forgotten my book. I returned to the cabin, carefully closing the door as I went in, got my book and went up to read for the next couple of hours.

When I got back Geoff was sitting on the bunk looking distraught. 'I've lost a cat,' he said.

'Lost a cat? How...? You can't have.'

'I have. I've looked everywhere. Polly is just not here.'

We turned the bunks inside out, looked underneath them, in the wardrobe, in the bathroom, everywhere. No Polly. She must have got out when I returned to fetch my book. But I'd been so careful.

'There's nothing for it,' said Geoff. 'I'll have to search the ship.' He then marched off, determined to seek out every nook and cranny.

The Patras–Venice ferry is big. In fact, it's huge. Hopeless. I sat on the edge of the bunk feeling dreadful. I started to pray.

'Heavenly Father,' I said, desperately, 'I know that in the grand scheme of things this is not very important, but please, please bring Polly back.'

Within seconds I heard a scratching from the bathroom. Kala was on the other bunk so it couldn't have been her. I opened the door and there was Polly, doing what she was supposed to do in the litter tray.

'Thank you, God. Thank you! Thank you!'

I grabbed her, put both kittens in the cat basket, shoved it in the wardrobe and wrote a hasty note to Geoff.

'Found Polly. Coming to find you. Mxx'

I knew that when, inevitably, he did not find Polly he would head straight for the purser's desk to confess. What would they do when they found out we had smuggled two cats into our cabin? I rushed to the purser's desk to waylay him and there he was striding towards it. I waved frantically.

'I've found her,' I hissed.

'Where?'

We made our way back to the cabin and started to try and work out where she had hidden in the bathroom. Eventually Geoff spotted a gap in the pipework under the sink, big enough to let Polly into the miles of ventilation winding its way round the ship. Thank God that she had needed a pee. We might have lost her forever and never known what had happened to her.

Laughing now that it was over, I asked Geoff if he'd been calling out 'Polly, Polly' in front of all the other passengers. No, he said, what he actually did was to tackle a bemused waiter with the word 'cattya, cattya' under the mistaken impression it was the word for cat. It isn't.

Early on the morning of day three we found ourselves in Venice and, carrying what was becoming an increasingly heavy cat basket between us, headed for the railway station. We could get an overnight train to Paris, via Bologna, at 6 p.m., with a private couchette (perfect for smuggling cats).

That meant we had a full day to kill in Venice, not normally much of a challenge but what to do with the kittens? What could we do but carry them around with us – all day. They were so good. Not a peep. Not a meow. And nowhere to let them out to feed or pee.

We boarded the train to Bologna on time and then connected to the extraordinarily long train to Paris just as the doors were closing, hopping into the last carriage. We were, inevitably, at the wrong end and started to make our way forwards.

Halfway along the conductor spotted us, looked at our tickets and said, '*Suivez-moi.*' Courteously he led us along corridor after corridor. I prayed that the kittens would keep quiet. Just as I started to breathe out with relief we heard pitiful mewing.

The conductor stopped and cocked an ear. My heart sank and then I heard my husband say, in a strange, falsetto voice, 'It's a very long way to the couchette, isn't it?'

The conductor gave him an alarmed look, slid back the couchette door and hurried away, leaving two thankful cat owners crying with laughter.

At the Gare du Nord we bought our train tickets and queued up to get on to the platform. No chance of smuggling them on board this time. The cases had to go through an X-ray machine, but that wouldn't be a problem. We had their passports. They were legal.

'*Les chats*,' I said, in my appalling French, indicating the cat basket. '*Pas le machine.*'

'Ai em sorry,' said the inspector. 'We do not allow ze animals on *Eurostar.*'

'But we've bought our tickets,' I said. He made a phone call and we were joined by a young man. We could not, he explained, take the kittens on *Eurostar*. Animals were not allowed. We would have to go to Calais and catch a ferry and he would book us on a train that would take us there. Also, we could not take the kittens on the ferry unless we were in a car. He explained where the nearest hire-car office was to the station at Calais and recommended that we take a taxi there, pick up a car and head for the port.

He spent an hour with us and even escorted us on to the train. (Perhaps he wanted to be sure we left?)

We were happy to hire a car as it meant we could drive home and leave it with Hertz in England. We presented our passports in Calais, boarded the ferry and drove through the 'Declare a Pet' section when we got to Dover. It was very late at night by this time and raining, if you'll forgive me, cats and dogs so there was no-one to check our papers.

And that, we thought, would be the end of it. The only problem now was what we were going to do with Polly and Kala when we returned to Greece the next summer. We would, we decided, take the car.

Mary Johns has been a print and broadcast journalist all her working life. A former presenter of a number of BBC One travel programmes including *Holiday*, *Perfect Holiday* and *Holiday 10 Best*, she was travel editor for BBC Hereford and Worcester and *BBC Parenting Magazine*. She is a former chairman  of the British Guild of Travel Writers and now spends her summers in Greece. Her first book, *Five Dogs, Two Cats and a Couple of Mugs* is available on Amazon.

Understanding Peggy

Hilary Bradt

'It's awfully small!' I said, looking in dismay at the nondescript brown pony tied to the gate with her sausage-shaped body, working-class tufts on her fetlocks and a silly hairstyle.

'She's perfect,' said Pedar, the horse dealer. 'Carry you all day. Never gets tired.' The pony couldn't have been more than 13.2 hands and I'm no midget.

'Don't you have anything else? Something bigger?' He shook his head. 'What's her name?'

'Peggy.'

So I saddled up and trotted up and down the road and cantered in the field.

'She's got very low head carriage,' I said snootily. This was putting it mildly; her neck was never above the horizontal.

Pedar stared. 'D'you want a show pony or a worker? She'll do you fine. I drive her all day in my gig.' Which explained the muscular neck, partially cropped mane to accommodate the collar, and brisk trot.

I really didn't like this pony. She was too small, too plain, and I couldn't forgive her for not being Mollie, my beautiful Connemara Mollie who had died halfway through my thousand-mile journey around the west of Ireland. No other pony was going to measure up. But there seemed to be no alternative, so the deal was done.

I took her for a longer ride before encumbering her with the saddlebags. When she felt soft turf beneath her hooves, instead of tarmac, Peggy stopped dead in surprise. Oh brave new world! Without her accustomed blinkers she could see mountains and sky – except that if she wanted to look at something above her she tilted her head sideways to peep under the imaginary blinkers while keeping her neck resolutely horizontal. It was endearing and made me laugh out loud. Her brown ears were so sharply pricked that they almost met in the middle, and I decided that perhaps she wasn't so bad.

Soon after we'd set out the next day Peggy was thrilled to see two horses ahead of her. We caught them up and I was less thrilled when the man leading them asked if I was going to Ballyferriter. I admitted that I was. 'Good, I'm tired, they can go with you,' and he turned them loose on the road. I refused to go along with his plan. The thought of being in charge of two loose horses on a busy narrow road for four miles didn't appeal to me. He exploded into a stream of curses. 'Go on, trot up the road!' he commanded. I walked and the loose horses investigated someone's drive. More oaths. So I trotted and they trotted behind until I slowed near a track leading into the mountains – obviously familiar territory to the horses, which cantered away out of sight. I was relieved to see them go. Peggy, however, was devastated. She neighed hopefully every five minutes or so throughout the day, and scanned the countryside for her new friends. Poor Peggy! I had taken her away from her home and companions, and I was learning that she was the most sociable pony I'd ever met. Depriving her of equine company made me feel permanently guilty.

Gradually Peggy and I got to know each other. She learned faster than I did, conveying her needs and wishes as eloquently as a pony can. I was very slow on the uptake. One day, instead of her usual brisk walk she dawdled along with her nose to the ground, smelling the tarmac and every now and then stopping to scrape it with her hoof. I couldn't think what the matter was. Then she spied a woman crossing her front garden carrying a bucket of water. Peggy raised her head and gave a little whinny. Of course! 'Would you mind giving my pony a drink?' I asked. The woman obligingly fetched a fresh bucket of cold water, and Peggy drank gratefully. She had already perfected the art of ensuring that I thought of her luncheon needs before mine. Generally I gave her an hour's break on the best grazing I could find, but sometimes the lure of a Guinness with my sandwich overcame my good manners. After I'd remounted she would dawdle along, stopping pointedly at likely-looking grass verges until I gave in. She also made it quite clear when she felt that my behaviour was insufferable. On one occasion when I was leading her to give us both a rest (so thoughtful), Peggy stopped suddenly. 'Come on, you stupid animal!' I said impatiently, hauling on the lead rope without looking back. Then I looked round and saw that the saddlebags had slipped sideways. Peggy turned her head and gave me such a hard stare that the memory still disturbs me. I apologised profusely and heaved them back into position. I swear that her lip curled triumphantly.

Peggy preferred to be on tarmac. Believing herself equal to any car when it came to roadwork, she considered rough terrain an unfair test for a harness pony. She approached hills like an inexperienced mountain climber, racing up for a dozen or so yards, then stopping to get her breath back. I tried to educate her into the proper mountaineer's plod, but she wasn't interested; it was much more satisfying to think up excuses for calling a halt. One that she soon perfected was stopping to evacuate her bowels. Fair enough, I thought, I wouldn't want to continue walking under those circumstances, so I let her pause. She quickly learned that by squeezing her droppings out one at a time she could stop as often as she chose. By the end of the trek I feared she'd do herself an internal injury by straining so hard.

I was learning Peggy language fast, but one thing I never quite grasped was how to recognise the right sort of grass. To me, grass is grass, and if it's succulent and green, then it's gourmet grass. Not to Peggy it wasn't and I refused to take notice of her when I had found what I considered the perfect camping place in a grassy clearing in a pine forest next to a stream. There was flat ground for the tent, running water and plenty of lovely green grass. Better still there was no need to tether Peggy in such an enclosed area.

Peggy's behaviour that evening was strange. Instead of settling down to graze, she showed an uncharacteristic interest in my activities. After a few mouthfuls of grass she stood by the luggage as though to say, 'OK, I'm ready to go now.' I ignored her and set up camp. Then she hung around putting her nose into everything, chewing the tent and my jacket, and paying particular attention to my soup cooking on the stove. I was afraid she'd burn herself (or knock over the soup) so pushed her away. Undeterred, she came back and I found her standing with a guy rope in her mouth dangling its tent peg. Still I chose not to get the message.

Next morning I was woken at six by Peggy stamping and snorting around the tent. My little room wobbled as she tripped over guy ropes and rubbed her chin along the flysheet. 'For heaven's sake go *away*!' I shouted. She did. I dozed in blessed silence for another hour and then unzipped the flap and looked out. I couldn't see her. She must be behind the tent near the river, I thought. I dressed, crawled out and looked around in increasing disbelief. Peggy had gone. A wave of sheer panic swept over me. Struggling to keep calm I considered the possibilities. Had she been stolen? It was possible, but unlikely in such a hidden spot and with my tent close by. I checked the area for hoof prints, and noticed that the ground had been disturbed around the path leading to the entrance gate; it looked as though she'd scrambled up the bank to get round the rope blocking her exit. There were fresh prints on the path and I guessed that she'd either jumped down on to the road or made her way through the pine trees to a large field. I pulled myself up the bank to the field, praying that she'd be there. She wasn't.

I was beside myself with anxiety. Suppose she was hit by a car? Or hurt in a dozen other ways? I thought she would probably head back to the stables where she'd enjoyed exceptional hospitality the day before, so started back along the road. It curved between high banks and I could never see more than a hundred yards ahead of me. Hopeless! My plan to flag down a passing car was pointless: there was no traffic on this minor road. I returned to the campsite to collect my binoculars and find a high point to survey the surrounding countryside. A herd of cows was grazing in a field about half a mile away. And among the black-and-white animals was a brown one. Could it be...? I jogged across to the bramble-covered bank that bordered the cow pasture and climbed up. There were the cows, and among the Friesians was one brown Hereford. I was bitterly disappointed. Of course, I should have realised that Peggy couldn't just join a herd of cows in an enclosed field. But then I saw her; she was standing by the fence watching me out of the corner of her eye as she stuffed herself with grass. Then she walked towards me with a little whinny.

If I had been unnerved by Peggy's adventure, she was transformed. Thereafter, I couldn't leave her for more than a few minutes before I would hear her neigh, and have to go out to reassure her that I still loved her, and promise that I would never tell her to go away again. Endearing though this was, it did put a dampener on some of my pleasures. I would just be settling down to my glass of Guinness when I'd hear pitiful neighs and have to finish my drink by her side. One time when I was enjoying a drink in the evening, knowing she was safe in an adjoining field next to my tent, I was called back by heart-rending sobs. I mean neighs. This time I thought she must be greeting another horse nearby, but no, she wanted me. So I had to forgo a second glass and return to the tent and write my diary by candlelight.

The journey ended in Limerick. After a holiday in a field with other horses for company, Pedar would take her back to Dingle to resume her job pulling his gig. She would sleep in the same field each night, with the same horse companions. Horses, like all animals, need routine to keep them happy.

I had taken Peggy out of her comfort zone and she had responded heroically. For want of other horses she had bonded with me, as I had with her. But it's taken over thirty years to appreciate just how much I owe her. When I started the trek I was still in the mindset that the most important part of horse management was control. Was the pony obedient? Could I make it do what I wanted? By the end of the journey I had learned that it was just as important for me to understand what the pony was trying to tell me. Peggy was the catalyst in that transition. With her sociable nature, trying to communicate with me came naturally to her. I am ashamed, now, at how slow I was to learn.

Hilary Bradt co-founded Bradt Travel Guides in 1974. In 1984 she rode through the west of Ireland first with Mollie, described in *Roam Alone*, then with Peggy. The journey is described in *Connemara Mollie* and *Dingle Peggy*, both published by Bradt.

From *Zarafa: A Giraffe's True Story, from Deep in Africa to the Heart of Paris*

Michael Allin

In 1826, the Ottoman Viceroy of Egypt, Muhammad Ali, was advised by the French consul general, Drovetti, to present King Charles X with a giraffe – the first ever to be seen in that country. The aim was to cement relations with France and forestall European intervention in his wars against the Greeks. Zarafa the young giraffe made an extraordinary journey of 3,500 miles from her original home in present-day Ethiopia, first strapped on to the back of a camel, then down the Nile to Alexandria and across the Mediterranean to Marseilles. From that southern port Zarafa walked to Paris, led by her devoted carers, through crowds numbering many thousands.

On the sea journey from Alexandria to Marseille, she was accompanied by two Arab handlers, Hassan and Atir, and three milk cows to provide her daily milk (she was not yet weaned) and sundry other gift animals.

A hole was cut in the deck of the brigantine to allow Zarafa to stand upright below. The edge of the hole was padded with straw to cushion impact to her neck in rolling seas. A canvas canopy was erected to protect her from sun and rain. Zarafa was shipped standing among the animals in the hold while her neck and head rode up with the humans on deck – an elegantly defining image, symbolic of the fact that, though her size and strength made her formidable, she was much more the honoured pet than a wild or even domesticated animal.

She spent the winter in Marseilles in a specially constructed stable, under the supervision of Etienne Geoffroy Saint-Hilaire, one of the foremost scientists of his time.

Now fifty-five and suffering from gout and rheumatism, Saint-Hilaire was a living legend, a grand and improbable eminence to make this journey with the giraffe on foot.

Marseilles to Paris in May and June of 1827 was a 550-mile parade, during which the giraffe became such a never-seen-before attraction that crowds rioted around her. People came out of their fields and vineyards and distant villages to marvel at this living mythological combination of creatures – a gentle and mysterious sort of horned camel whose hump had been straightened by stretching its neck, with legs as tall as a man and the cloven hoofs of a cow, and markings like a leopard or a maze of lightning, and that startling blue-black snake of a twenty-inch tongue.

When they reached Paris, Saint-Hilaire's only comment was his loving official report:

'The health of the animals was in no way altered during the journey; on the contrary, their health is notably strengthened. A female mouflon lambed at Lapalud and the baby well-endured the journey.

'But it is principally the Giraffe whom the journey has marvellously benefited. She gained weight and much more strength from the exercise: her muscles were more defined, her coat smoother and glossier upon her arrival here than they were in Marseilles: she is presently 12'2 tall. Also during the journey, her ways became more trusting: she no longer refuses to drink in front of strangers; and her complacency with the play of the little mouflon, which [while resting off her feet, the giraffe] accepted on her back, testifies that she is as debonair as she is intelligent.'

After being received by the king, Zarafa was put on daily exhibition at le Jardin des Plantes. In the last three weeks of July 1827, sixty thousand people came to see her. She was soon the subject of songs and instrumental music, poems and music-hall sketches, and anonymous political satires criticising the king's censorship of the press. Paris adored her.

Atir remained in Paris with Zarafa, becoming renowned as the Arab who lived with the giraffe in her enclosure at the Jardin des Plantes. Two ladders took him up to a mezzanine where he slept within scratching reach of her head. Grooming her was his daily public performance.

Michael Allin has worn out five passports writing movies and researching books in North and South America, Europe, Asia and Africa.

One Man and a Mule

Hugh Thomson

The idea of taking a mule across England had come about in the same focused way as so many of my projects: some long-entertained half-thought (like trying to find an Inca ruin or running a black-market car from Texas to Central America) crystallising into action without at any stage being examined for plausibility, possibility, or sheer bloody stupidity.

I'd worked a lot with mules as pack animals in Peru and thought it would be intriguing to do the same along the rough route of the Coast to Coast, although obviously I would need to take bridleways not footpaths. So I found a mule called Jethro at an RSPCA rescue centre.

As soon as I met him, I could see Jethro had a bit of a spare tyre. If anything, this made me sympathetic. Just another middle-aged mule/male. Moreover, Jethro had been gelded late in life, so retained the energies and inclinations, if not the abilities, of a stallion.

He was small – about twelve-and-a-half hands – with striking colouring, a freckling of white and beige like an appaloosa, and an enquiring and appraising gaze which I came to learn was characteristic. Our first meeting in the stable yard at the RSPCA was cordial, if not effusive; so English in the best possible sense. I noticed his eyes: dark, soulful and thoughtful. His unusual colouring was not like anything I had seen in Peru, where mules tended to come either bay or skewbald.

Alice, one of his RSPCA carers, told me: 'The thing about Jethro, is that he either likes you or he doesn't.'

This seemed straightforward; and Jethro had so far showed no sign of taking against me.

'The other thing is… he's very intelligent. He'll only do something if he wants.'

Alice's tone implied that Jethro's intelligence was not always a helpful quality.

We had two hundred miles ahead of us to test this out. What with the problems with the bridleways as well, it was going to be an interesting, but challenging, journey.

Together with an Irish friend of mine called Jasper Winn who had a lot of experience of muleteering, we set off from St Bees. On reaching the Lakes, I wanted to take Jethro along the old pack-pony path that wound from the Honister quarries towards the ring of mountains of the Western Fells, centred on the domed anvil of Great Gable. The path was called 'Moses' Trod' after a nineteenth-century quarryman who designed the route to contour beautifully around the slope ahead of us and run for some fifteen miles across the Western Fells, through Wasdale Head, before arriving at Ravenglass for the ships.

We were only a little into the journey, yet Jethro was already walking quietly and calmly as we set off from the quarry op; his ears set back, he looked engaged and interested. Jasper thought he had already lost a bit of weight. His cinches were fitting better and he was a smartly turned out mule as well, in a striped Colorado riding blanket with some leather saddlebags.

Not that the saddlebags were carrying much. Jethro was unwilling to bear much of a load, which was clearly a problem given he was meant to be a pack animal. He had the smallest saddlebags I'd ever seen on a mule: no bigger than the clutch bags carried by ladies who lunch. We were, as we pointed out to him occasionally, carrying far more on our own backs. He would never have made the grade carrying slate along the path, back in the day.

'So if we let him loose now when we were having a picnic, would he just take off or hang around?' I wondered idly to Jasper.

'He wouldn't take off at all. He's decided we're his herd. Not a very pleasant herd, and decidedly lacking in intelligence, with terrible ears, but about as good as he's going to get, so he's making the best of it.'

For a late-October day it was unseasonably mild and sunny, giving us views of the sea through the gaps in the mountains. Wordsworth always claimed that October was the best month in the lakes. To the north, I could even make out the faint glimmer of wind farms far offshore in the Atlantic.

Jethro chose that moment to wake me up from my contemplation by bolting sharply. Quite what alarmed him, I'm not sure; nor was this the first or last time it happened. It may have been a walker with a dog who was approaching and was now amused to see two grown men running after the rope trailing behind Jethro, like balloonists who had lost their balloon.

'You need to keep that donkey under control,' he said helpfully, with a laugh.

Jasper and I were too out of breath to respond.

A little later that day, despite having walked and run this route many times, and even with the Wainwright guide to hand, I managed to get lost contouring around Moses' Trod. The paths had divided over the years, without the cohesion any more of being a pack-pony route.

Humans are more prone to wander than animals led in teams. Or at least, that was my excuse.

In my defence – as I pointed out to Jasper, who at this early stage in the walk still assumed I might know what I was doing – the route had changed in many places to negotiate a newly strengthened boundary fence, which in the old days, as Wainwright attested, was broken and not much of an obstacle. Indeed, the boundary fence was a rude reminder of something I had managed so far wilfully to ignore. Despite the fact that Moses' Trod had always been a bridleway in the past, constructed for pack ponies, it had now reverted to footpath status; so when we came to the boundary fence, there was a quite legitimate – and impassable – stile. This was something we would encounter right along our journey.

Jasper and I discussed how many obstacles we had already come across in trying to get a mule across the countryside. For I was beginning to realise that to take a pack animal across England, which once would have been so natural as to attract no notice, was now working against the lie of the land; that the route was bifurcated with everything from stiles to boundary fences to the six lanes of the M6. The process of enclosure, begun so controversially in the eighteenth century, was still continuing.

It was still a strange thing to be travelling across England with a mule. Strange because while once the whole landscape would have been filled with pack animals and it would have been unusual to meet anyone who wasn't carrying goods, now these drovers' roads were like motorways without any cars.

And that also made it exhilarating: the sense of reanimating a landscape. Already I found the way that Jethro pulled us along – or held us back – gave a different rhythm to the way I walked. I was enjoying the difference.

A few days later, I found myself doing a radio interview with Radio Cumbria for their breakfast show, as they had heard I was crossing their county.

'That was "Mule Train" by Bo Diddley. And there's a reason for playing it because on the line we have Hugh Thomson, who has taken it upon himself to walk through Cumbria with a mule. And then Yorkshire as well, but we're not so interested in that, are we?'

'So, Hugh, how does it work? Are you riding the mule?'

I was getting practised at this particular answer by now: 'No, he's just a pack animal. And his name's Jethro.' I bridled at him being referred to as 'the mule'. Jethro was a name not a number.

'OK. So Jethro carries everything, does he? Your tent and everything. Your *supplies*.'

As has already been duly recorded, Jethro carried so little it was embarrassing. Our standard muleteers' lunch. Perhaps some water. And the symbolic three pebbles for each of us Jasper had loaded on the beach at St Bees. But it felt disloyal to let him down in public.

'Well, that's the idea...'

'So what gave you the idea for this? I mean, it seems a very odd thing to do, isn't it?'

'Maybe. But I've travelled a lot in Peru, where they use mules a great deal, and I really enjoyed walking with them. So I thought why not do it back home and explore some of the old pack-animal routes that cross the north of England.'

'Best of luck, Hugh. I hope listeners will carry a carrot in their pockets, just in case they meet you. And let me ask something that everyone else will – have you bonded with Jethro yet?'

This was a good question. And also the last. I replied as well as I could ('It's early days' or something to that effect) but realised I needed to answer it for myself.

I wandered out to see Jethro in the field where he had been spending the night. He did his usual trick of standing sideways so he could keep me in vision without having to acknowledge that he was doing so.

In some ways, looking after Jethro was like having a teenager – and given I had three teenage children of my own and two teenage stepdaughters, I felt well qualified on this subject. You can spend weeks with a teenager and get no response, love or thanks; but precisely because of that, when you do, it's so unexpected, it can feel like an almost sublime moment of transfiguration.

I knew Jethro had been through a troubled past. Although the RSPCA were circumspect, I had learned that in his original home, before they rescued him, he was unloved and misunderstood. Enough to make any teenager rebellious. As so often, it sounded as if he had been the unwanted consequence of leaving a donkey in a field with a mare. Just as the English had such startling levels of teenage pregnancies due to lack of sex education, so they seemed blithely unaware that donkeys could procreate with horses. And the result would be a mule. Given all the ignorance and prejudice about mules – that they were stubborn and hard to deal with – it was not surprising that Jethro could be difficult at times. It was more surprising that at times he wasn't.

Jasper had been patiently teaching me the business of muleteering: from setting up the electric fence at each place we stopped to how to box him into the horse lorry. But one thing I didn't enjoy was having to catch Jethro, which was what needed to happen now. Despite weeks of training at home and on the road, this wasn't getting any easier.

Usually I was the sous-chef in this particular operation. Jasper would hold out a bucket of pony nuts and make peculiar noises that sounded like Mongolian throat singing. We would then both close on Jethro until he consented to let Jasper attach the lead rope.

Today, however, he got bored of the usual procedure and trotted over to me meekly to present his neck. It was one of those rare moments when we had indeed bonded.

One Man and a Mule is published by Penguin Random House. **Hugh Thomson**'s other books include *The Green Road into the Trees*, which won the inaugural Wainwright Prize for best travel and nature writing.

Hedgehogs on the Road

Tanis Jordan

All our rescue hedgehogs had been farmed out to carers, the last bottle of wine was stowed in our VW van cupboard along with pillows and duvet. At last we were ready to go, our first break of the year.

Then the phone rang and my heart sank as I heard the words, 'I've been given your number...'

As hedgehog rehabilitators, that familiar introduction usually meant one thing, and tonight was no exception.

'Is that the hedgehog lady?' said a desperate-sounding voice. 'I've got six baby hedgehogs running around on my patio. What shall I do?'

'Can you catch them and put them in a box?'

'Yes, but what then? What shall I do with them?'

'Would you like us to take them?' I responded automatically.

'Oooh, yes please.'

For more than twenty-five years we've never turned an animal away. Some years we release more than a hundred. My husband Martin filled a hot-water bottle to keep them warm while being collected. Warmth is truly the very 'first aid' for young or poorly hedgehogs.

Soon we had a huddle of tiny hoglets warming up nicely and obviously very hungry. They looked about three to four weeks old, and we expected they would eat Pedigree Chum puppy food mashed up with some Esbilac puppy milk. But when presented with a dish of mash they behaved as if they'd never encountered solid food before.

One sniffed some of it straight up its nose and began sneezing; one tried to kill it by diving into it; the biggest hog stamped straight across it, the smallest sat in the middle of it as another clambered over him and the sixth hog showed no interest at all. Nobody ate anything.

'They need hand feeding!' Martin sighed. 'I'll fetch a pipette.'

'And toileting first!' I added. In the wild, their mum would give them a quick lick to stimulate bowel and bladder action, but I was not *that* dedicated. I preferred to tickle their bits with a tissue until they went.

Soon, one by one, they were toileted and fed, then popped under their blanket till the morning. What to do with them now? No real choice, we agreed. They'd have to come with us in the campervan.

They were small enough to live together in the same cage. So, next morning, we packed powdered puppy milk, tins of puppy food, dishes, pipettes, heat pads, hot-water bottles and fleecy blankets and with our three-legged hedgehog called 'Tripod', we set off for the wilds of Pembrokeshire.

We'd rescued Tripod when he was just about to expire. A broken hip, a broken toe, the worst mite infestation the vet had ever seen, a bad case of lungworm, and a smashed leg that had to come off. With the amputation he'd cost us a fortune in vets' bills, but he was worth it. A gentle, lovely animal who seemed to enjoy life to the full, though he could never be released into the wild as he'd be too vulnerable.

At the site we checked in.

'Just the two of you?'

'Yep.'

'No animals – dogs or cats?'

'Er, no.' Surely baby hedgehogs didn't count and Tripod only counted as about seventy-five per cent.

We found a pitch and put up the awning as a freezing gale blew in from the sea.

'It'll be hard keeping this lot warm,' Martin commented, as the awning billowed and attempted to turn itself inside out and rain poured down the windows. We offloaded everything we didn't need into the awning, plugged in the hoglets' heat pad and put the kettle on. Soon, we were steaming up nicely, and the hoglets were warm and comfortable. Tripod, one of the most relaxed animals ever, slept in his cage in the footwell, snorting and snuffling, no doubt dreaming of dinners to come. Soon the hoglets were hungry. They squeaked, they scratched, they climbed over each other and nibbled our fingers, demanding food.

One by one we toileted and fed them, until we came to the last one. She refused everything, huffing and puffing and prickling up her needle-sharp spines. As fast as Martin fed her, she spat the food out of the side of her mouth until both of them were covered in milky mash. There's always one! we agreed.

Night came.

'It's too cold outside for Tripod,' Martin announced. 'He can stay inside.'

'He's a hedgehog, Martin. He'll be fine in the awning.'

'Yes, but...'

He stayed inside.

Later, after a couple of glasses of wine, we settled down to sleep, just as the hedgehogs woke up. The hoglets sneezed and snuffled gently as they explored their house. I'd forgotten Tripod's habit of farting gently all night in between scratching up the paper to make himself a nest. And how he enjoyed turning his empty metal food dish over and over so it clanked against the floor.

Next morning the wind had dropped, the sun shone and it was getting warm. After toast and coffee we started on the hogs. Hedgehog rehabbers are obsessed by poo; it's a wonderful guide to the health of the animal and we were delighted to see little patches of pale-green poo dotted about the hoglets' cage, a sure sign that their bowels were functioning properly. Everybody fed well apart from the 'one' whose tiny, beady eyes glared at Martin as she dribbled her food down his T-shirt.

We noted their weight in a book. Weight is important for tiny animals; a gradual gain of three grams a day is great, but the same amount lost can spell the end within a few days.

The one thing we had to do according to friends and relatives, who all seemed to know, was to make a trip to 'The Shed', boldly claimed to be the best place for fish and chips in the whole of Wales. By mid-morning when we got on our bikes it was very warm indeed.

'This feels like Spain,' Martin observed, as we pedalled along empty lanes bordered by grass verges rich with wildflowers.

An hour later we stopped to drink some water and check the map.

'They said it was only about fifteen minutes away,' I puffed.

'Yeah,' Martin agreed. 'It probably is – by car!'

It was a beautiful ride, but we were both knackered when we arrived.

We slid into a booth and ordered a couple of ice-cold beers as we waited for our food.

'Those hoglets are doing well,' Martin commented.

'Mmm, they won't be too hot, will they?'

'No, they'll be fine.'

'Good. Did we leave a window open?' I mused, munching on a chip.

'No, do you think we should have?'

'Well, the roof's open so air can circulate.'

'But they're on a heat pad as well, and it *is* very hot,' said Martin, looking worried.

'They'll be OK, though, won't they?' I said, as we finished our meal.

'We'd better get back!' we said together.

In the heat of the boiling afternoon we pedalled back, sweat pouring from us and heatstroke an imminent danger. Waves of guilt wafted over us as we imagined finding six limp bodies.

As we raced into the site our dramatic entrance drew stares from the other campers. We flung down our bikes and opened the door of the van. Six little bodies lay sleeping soundly, a bit hot and sticky, but nothing to worry about.

'Hello, everything alright?' The couple from the van next door stood there, looking concerned.

'We've got some baby hedgehogs in here and we were worried they might get too hot,' I explained.

'Hedgehogs!' said the wife. 'I've never seen a live hedgehog.'

They were completely enthralled by the babies. Tripod didn't get a look in.

Over the next few days our journeys were planned around the hoglets. At each feeding time we had an audience of happy campers taking photos and videos of them. On the evening of the day before we were due to leave, feeding time was progressing as normal. After feeding, the babies were placed into a clean cage and tucked under a fleecy blanket.

'That's number five toileted and fed,' said Martin, as he filled the pipette.

'Let's have number six.'

I checked the cage. It was empty. I searched through the used paper and cloths; *surely I hadn't chucked the baby out by mistake*? No, of course not.

'It's gone!' I said.

'What do you mean, *gone*?' Martin said. 'Where's it gone?'

'It's got out,' I said. Hedgehogs are notorious escapees, but it was so tiny. How had the hoglet got out? Simple. There was a hole in the cage to carry it by, too high off the floor for an unaided hoglet, but not too high for an enterprising animal clambering on top of a snoozing heap of its brothers and sisters! The next thing to establish was whether or not the hoglet was still inside the van. Ten minutes of crawling around on our hands and knees, examining every inch of floor and wall, convinced us that there was nowhere it could have got out. More fruitless searching ensued; then I had an inspiration. I picked up the plastic bag containing all our dirty washing and tipped everything out on to the seat.

There was our missing hedgehog tucked away inside one of Martin's dirty socks, fast asleep.

Two months later and our litter of six tiny hoglets had reached a combined weight in excess of three kilograms and were duly released into the wilds of the South Shropshire hills. We can never know, of course, how they're doing in their new life of freedom, but we'd like to believe they're all well and leading productive hedgehog lives. And one thing is certain: they'll never get another luxury, family, full-board campervan holiday in Wales.

Tanis Jordan spent decades making expeditions in South America with her husband Martin, with whom she co-wrote two travel books (one in 1982 for the newly formed Bradt Enterprises) and four lavish picture  books about South America. She has had seven children's novels published. They live in Shropshire and run a nature reserve and a hedgehog sanctuary.

From *The Bible in Spain*

George Borrow

George Borrow travelled through Spain between 1835 and 1840 distributing Bibles for the British and Foreign Bible Society. Spain was at that time a turbulent country following the Napoleonic Wars, and Borrow travelled deep into the countryside.

I would I were a wolf,' said one of the shepherds; 'or, indeed, anything rather than what I am... He fares better and is more respected than the wretch of a shepherd.'

'A dangerous person is the wolf,' said the other shepherd, 'and cunning as dangerous; who knows more than he? He knows the vulnerable point of every animal; see, for example, how he flies at the neck of a bullock, tearing open the veins with his grim teeth and claws. But does he attack a horse in this manner? I trow not.'

'Not he,' said the other shepherd; 'he is too good a judge but he fastens on the haunches, and hamstrings him in a moment. Oh the fear of the horse when he comes near the dwelling of the wolf. My master was the other day riding in the *despoblado*, above the pass, on his fine Andalusian steed, which had cost him five hundred dollars; suddenly the horse stopped, and sweated and trembled like a woman in the act of fainting; my master could not conceive the reason but presently he heard a squealing and growling in the bushes, whereupon he fired off his gun and scared the wolves, who scampered away; but he tells me that the horse has not yet recovered from his fright.'

'Yet the mares know, occasionally, how to balk him,' replied his companion; 'there is great craft and malice in mares as there is in all females; see them feeding in the *campo* with their young *cría* about them; presently the alarm is given that the wolf is drawing near; they start wildly and run about for a moment, but it is only for a moment – again they gather together, forming themselves into a circle, in the centre of which they place the foals. Onward comes the wolf, hoping to make his dinner on horseflesh; he is mistaken, however – the mares have balked him, and are as cunning as himself. Not a tail is to be seen – not a hinder quarter – but there stand the whole troop, their fronts towards him ready to receive him, and as he runs around them barking and howling they rise successively on their hind legs, ready to stamp him to the earth, should he attempt to hurt their cría or themselves.'

'Did I not hear your worship say that you wished to buy a horse?' said the gipsy.

'I do not want to buy a horse,' said I, 'if I need anything it is a pony to carry our baggage; but it is getting late. Antonio, pay the reckoning.'

'Stay, your worship, do not be in a hurry,' said the gipsy, 'I have got the very pony which will suit you.'

Without waiting for my answer he hurried into the stable from whence he presently returned, leading an animal by the halter. It was a pony of about thirteen hands high, of a dark red colour; it was very much galled all over, the marks of ropes and thongs being visible on its hide. The figure, however, was good, and there was an extraordinary brightness in its eye.

'There, your worship,' said the gipsy; 'there is the best pony in all Spain.'

'He looks feeble,' said I, 'his work is well-nigh done.'

'Feeble as he is, *Señor*, you could not manage him; no, nor any Englishman in Spain.'

I looked at the creature again, and was still more struck with its figure. I was in need of a pony to relieve occasionally the horse of Antonio in carrying the baggage which we had brought from Madrid, and though the condition of this was wretched, I thought that by kind treatment I might possibly soon bring him round.

'May I mount this animal?' I demanded.

'He is a baggage pony, Señor, and is ill to mount. He will suffer none but myself to mount him, who am his master. When he once commences running, nothing will stop him but the sea. He springs over hills and mountains, and leaves them behind in a moment. If you will mount him, Señor, suffer me to fetch a bridle, for you can never hold him in with the halter.'

'This is nonsense,' said I. 'You pretend that he is spirited in order to enhance the price. I tell you his work is done.'

I took the halter in my hand and mounted. I was no sooner on his back than the creature, who had before stood stone still, without displaying the slightest inclination to move and who in fact gave no further indication of existence than occasionally rolling his eyes and pricking up an ear, sprang forward like a racehorse, at a most desperate gallop. I had expected that he might kick or fling himself down on the ground in order to get rid of his burden, but for this escapade I was quite unprepared. I had no difficulty in keeping on his back, having been accustomed from my childhood to ride without a saddle. To stop him, however, baffled all my endeavours, and I almost began to pay credit to the words of the gipsy who had said that he would run on until he reached the sea. I had a strong arm, and tugged at the halter until I compelled him to turn slightly his neck, which from its stiffness might almost have been of wood; yet he did not abate his speed for a moment. On the left side of the road down which he dashed was a deep trench, just where the road took a turn towards the right, and over this he sprang in a sideward direction; the halter broke with the effort, the pony shot forward like an arrow, while I fell back into the dust.

George Borrow (1803–81) was born in Norfolk, England. His account of five years in Spain became a bestseller, and he went on to publish three more travel tales. He was a great linguist and is admired for his writings on the Romany or Gypsies. He was also a great horseman and walker.

The Show Must Go On

Sarah Pope

'I propose a toast. To the English musicians!'

Felix stared at the vodka bottle. 'It's full of goldfish!'

Galya shook her head, and poured three shots, fast. '*Nyet*! No fish!' It was spiked with red chillies.

'Tomorrow you play like romantic Russians. No more polite English violinists. Welcome to Russian Christmas Orchestra tour UK.' Galya was the tour manager.

Felix and I were last-minute substitutes in the Russian Christmas Orchestra. We had never met before. It was the start of two weeks on the festive road, taking in Wolverhampton, Glasgow, Leeds and Margate.

All day, we'd been rehearsing *Nutcracker Fun*, like mice in a maze: 'Too fast, too quiet, too loud, too Brexit, you have played a wrong note…' The musical director tried to make us into romantic Russians, while the keyboard player complained that his hands couldn't be expected to perform the 'Dance of the Sugar Plum Fairy' solo in this very cold theatre. 'Russian cold good. English cold bad.'

Now we were sitting on Galya's bed, in her budget Earl's Court hotel room, waiting for the smokers to come in from the English cold. They were making the most of their duty-frees, out in the bus shelter under the Christmas lights. The whole neighbourhood pulsed with orange angels and reeked of Golden Fleece filter tips.

A black holdall, the size of a donkey, blocked the bathroom, where more bottles were cooling. Galya unzipped a corner to extract a framed photo from the company provisions. Nobody planned to spend their subsistence allowance on food, so Galya kept the holdall stocked with tinned fish, Russian salad and duty-frees, along with the company paperwork and music library.

'See,' said Galya, 'The two stupid Mr Stradivarius talk to Mr Sugar Plum Fairy.'

It was a publicity shot of two white-tie-and-tails violinists we didn't recognise, posing with today's Sugar Plum Fairy keyboard soloist, in his white-ruff collar and cuffs.

'Maestro Cold Finger himself! Look at those frills,' said Felix.

'The two Mr Stradivarius, who do not listen to advice from UK Foreign Office,' Galya shrugged, and kissed the picture, 'So *you* are here, in their place, English violinists. Welcome.'

Apparently, the two Mr Stradivarius had infringed the new international eco-legislation. Border Force at Heathrow had impounded their priceless eighteenth-century violins, because they were decorated with 'endangered species' Brazilian rosewood and ivory. The two were probably still at the airport, arguing with security.

'Now they must buy new *sustainable* violins, made in China, for tour,' said Galya, 'and we must pay young polite violinists, made in England, until they return.'

She set the chillies swimming and poured another round.

'Shall I... call... for a take-away?' But Felix fell asleep, head slumped on my shoulder, before he could find his phone.

'Two problems,' said Galya.

She was sitting beside me on the overheated orchestra coach to Wolverhampton, her feet on the donkey-sized holdall. Every now and then, someone asked the driver to turn the heating up or down, and the music off. I was trying to sleep. It was 7.30 a.m. and the M40 was crawling with holiday traffic. There was a suspicion of Golden Fleece in the air. Galya shook my arm to make sure I was awake.

'Problem one: pianist has cold hands. Problem two: we must buy… small… animal. I don't know his name. Now I need your help.'

'Google it?' Felix popped up, bright-eyed and functioning, from the seat behind, searching for his phone.

Galya poked around in the holdall and found her grandmother's legacy phrase book. No roaming charges there. Felix looked over her shoulder as she read:

'Please… give me a three-pence piece for this phone… nyet…'

She whizzed through the pages. 'Yes, Domestic Animals: 'Take me to the kangaroo paddocks… nyet… I have a pet dog, bird, reptile, rabbit… nyet…'

'Go on, you have a google.' Felix handed her *my* phone.

'Felix!'

Heads together, they scrolled through Popular Pet Animals. 'Mouse, rat, hamster, chinchilla, gerbil, ferret, jonny pig. Yes. We buy this… jonny pig.'

'Jonny pig? Guinea pig, gui-nea-pig, Galya,' Felix pronounced it for her, 'Why?'

'Mr Vadim Sugar Plum, solo *celeste* keyboard player, has always cold fingers. He takes this warm animal in his hands during intermission to prepare for Sugar Plum Fairy solo performance in part two of concert. Mr Aleksey Stradivarius, is jonny pig 'father'. Always the animal lives in his coat. Mr Boris Stradivarius, his friend, finds food for jonny pig. Now we have lost the two Mr Stradivarius, and jonny pig, at airport.'

'Gui-nea-pig, Galya,' said Felix.

'First we must buy new animal. If no guinea pig, Maestro Vadim cannot play very famous Sugar Plum solo. Stiff hands. Children cry, bad review, no more tour, no pay…'

I could mind-read Galya. She was grooming us to become guinea pig 'father' and 'feeder'.

'What do they eat?' Felix asked, on the same wavelength.

Galya found some stock images of a 'prizewinner' rosette-haired, black guinea pig, with white moustache, ankle and collar markings, labelled 'First in Class'.

'Give it a cigarette, and it would be a dead ringer for Mr Sugar Plum, Cold Finger, in his concert clothes,' said Felix. 'Do you think it won the prize for piano playing?'

The morning market was packing up when we got to Wolverhampton City Centre. Galya pleaded with the coach driver to let us out at the lights. We grabbed our violin cases and helped drag the holdall across the dual carriageway.

'Do you do requests, luv?' A stallholder offered Galya a satsuma as we picked our way through his crates. He took in her style with a quick head-to-toe glance – purple leggings and a real mink coat.

'Where can I buy a jonny pig?' Galya asked him, looking around the desolate site. His eyebrows disappeared under his baseball cap and he blew on his half-mittened fingers. Bits of cabbage and Christmas wrapping whirled past.

'It's not that sort of market, luv,' he said. 'Where you from? Give us a tune, will ya?'

'Guinea pig. We need to buy a guinea pig. Where's the pet stall?' Felix sounded stressed. It was starting to rain.

'You want Max,' called out the girl in plastic antlers, from the fabric stall opposite. 'He'll be here Saturday for the Christmas crowd. He deals exotics and family pets.' She patted a leopard-spotted curtain length. 'I'll text you his number. He'll be in the shop now and tomorrow.'

We still had half an hour before the rehearsal.

'Guinea pig or lunch?' I said.

'Guinea pig burger,' said Felix. 'I can do the shopping with Mr Sugar Plum tomorrow before the show. He knows what he wants. Big and warm.'

'What have you done, Felix!'

My violin case was next to his on the civic hall band room table. We had come off stage for the interval of the first show. I shrieked as I opened the case. It was occupied. A beautiful, bedraggled black-and-white guinea pig and three babies! And a bowl of carrot sticks from the bar. And a terrible stink. They were tucked up in my Thai silk wrap. The babies were exact replicas of their mother, in black with white ruffles. They looked like choristers.

'Babies!' said Felix. 'Buy one, get three free.'

Galya was wringing her hands. 'Men shopping!' she said, in the direction of Felix.

'Vadim said, "Get the big one. We call him Pushkin. Big is warm. Big is beautiful."' Felix stroked the mother's nose. She started squealing and the babies joined in.

'Big was pregnant,' I said. 'It's *Mrs* Pushkin.'

'Two problems,' said Galya. 'Problem one: Vadim must take Mrs Pushkin in his hands now to prepare for Sugar Plum solo, but Mrs Pushkin cries when she cannot see babies. Must be silent on stage. Problem two: babies cold and hungry when no mother.'

Vadim picked up the guinea pig mother and she began her distress call, squirming and biting. Felix took her from Vadim and dropped her into my velvet handbag. Vadim sucked blood off his thumb.

'There you go. Look after Mrs Pushkin for Vadim,' Felix said to me.

I was still holding my violin, with the velvet bag hanging on my shoulder, so I couldn't resist. Felix picked up the babies in the damp, sticky silk wrap, and tucked them into my bag with their mother. The squealing stopped.

We went back on stage. Fortunately my chair was just in front of Mr Sugar Plum at the keyboard. I rested the violin on the floor and opened my handbag with care. The musical director raised his baton and glared. He waited, transfixed, while I lifted the sticky, writhing bundle into Mr Sugar Plum's grasp. In the breathless audience silence before the first note, a handful of carrots clattered on to the stage.

'Three problems,' said Galya after the show, in my hotel room, feeding dilute condensed milk to Mrs Pushkin with a spoon. The dish appeared to be full of goldfish. Felix had dropped the spare carrots into it. We were waiting for the smokers to join us.

'Problem one: Mrs Pushkin does not like music.'

'Yeah, makes her pee,' said Felix. 'At least it's warm, to start with.'

'Problem Two: Mr Sugar Plum cannot play with wet hands.'

Mr Sugar Plum was helping himself to my towel in the bathroom.

'Problem Three: musical director does not like English musicians. He says no discipline, not polite. Special rehearsal for English musicians in Glasgow tomorrow.'

At that moment, the smokers burst in with fish and chips, and a can of dog food for Mrs Pushkin and family.

'Don't give her that. They don't eat meat,' I said.

'We can get a dog in Glasgow,' said Felix, showing Vadim a map of Scotland on his phone. 'Tomorrow, Scotland, very cold country. We shall all need guinea pigs. Only five hours from here by coach. The Scots will be practising "Auld Lang Syne" on the bagpipes, ready for New Year.'

'I propose a toast. To the English musicians,' said Mr Sugar Plum, appearing from the bathroom with my towel round his shoulders. He shook Felix by the hand and helped himself to the vodka.

'Tomorrow, whisky,' said Felix, stroking Mrs Pushkin in her nest of my pillows. She began squealing. The babies joined in.

'Mrs Pushkin not like vodka,' said Vadim, offering her his glass. 'Maybe she prefer whisky. Tomorrow she will sleep in concert.'

The squealing crescendo-ed. There was a tap at the door. I was psyched up for the no-pet-policy directive from hotel security. Almost as bad, there stood the musical director with a plastic bag.

'This is for you.' It was the first time we had seen him smile. Mr Sugar Plum Vadim must have put in a word for us.

'It's for *you*, Mrs Pushkin!' Felix was tearing into the twelve-litre pack of Extra Select Meadow Hay – 'a loose, unchopped, dust-extracted blend of grasses from chemical-free pastures'.

'I propose a toast, to the English guinea pig,' said the musical director, offering Mrs Pushkin a handful of luxury hay. The whole family squealed with excitement.

Sarah Pope has travelled the world as a viola player in symphony orchestras and played with her string quartet for pizza restaurants, Mediterranean cruises and the Savoy Hotel. She has written reviews and features for music magazines and a violin book for beginners entitled *A New Tune A Day*.

Lost and Found in the Arctic

Kelsey Camacho

That day, the blizzard was so strong that I couldn't tell whether we were moving or standing still. There was so much snow and wind smearing the landscape that I could barely see my lead dog five metres in front of me. The dogs had collected a layer of ice and snow on their fur, so it almost seemed like they were being erased. They kept their ears back, tails down as they focused on pulling forward. It was only two in the afternoon, but everything was dark – the sun still absent in January, never rising above the southern horizon. That day, we were in the middle of a smudged chalkboard that never stopped expanding.

I was on Svalbard, the archipelago halfway between Norway and the North Pole. I was guiding an overnight expedition on dogsled, with a couple from London and eighteen dogs. The previous night, we had camped on top of a mountain a few valleys away. Setting everything up was the easy part: anchoring the dogs in a circle around the tent to act as polar bear guards, tossing them blocks of meat for dinner, starting a fire, digging a toilet. We had spent the evening drinking tea and talking about how each of us ended up on this vacant edge of the earth, while the weather outside the tent lost its mind. The conditions were always unpredictable this time of year – gale-force winds ripping through the valleys at one minute, silence the next. A landscape so still that even breathing seemed disruptive.

The difficult part was finding our way home. When we left camp, the weather was calm with clear visibility, even for the polar night. The sky still held that deep shade of twilight – the 'blue hour', as the northerners call it. I coasted down the mountain with my two guests behind me, each of us in control of our sleds during the steep downhill parts. No-one flipped or lost their dogs. So far, so good. There were only ten kilometres to go until we reached the kennel.

I was glad that I had brought Carmen as my lead dog; she was one of the most experienced dogs in the yard, and always held a stoic expression. She was calm, brave and confident in her direction. While all the other dogs barked and jumped and howled before running, she always lay down and quivered, staring straight ahead at whatever path we were taking. It was as if she was looking the unknown straight in the eye.

Everything turned once we entered Adventdalen, the wide valley we had to cross in order to make it back to the kennel. It was a sprawling riverbed that was frozen for the winter, but the weather was notoriously terrible there; all of the wind seemed to funnel through that valley. Because of how wide it was, white-out conditions and poor visibility were common.

In some stretches of tundra, the wind had blown away all the snow, leaving bare sheets of ice and rock jutting from the ground. I held tightly to the sled, shifting my weight to avoid tipping over. *Like driving a dogsled on the moon*, I thought. At that moment, we could have been a million miles from anything.

Eventually we passed the two iron beds abandoned in the middle of the valley, standing in the dark like ghosts. They were left behind years ago by people who were renovating their cabins in the spring. On their way to town, they had discovered the river had opened up due to the snow melting. They left the beds there to get rid of extra weight slowing them down, and the beds have served as a local landmark ever since. Once I saw them, I knew we were headed in the right direction. It was basically a straight shot home from here.

It felt like we had been going in the same direction for an hour when I saw it – the tall cabin that marked the far side of the valley, directly opposite the kennel. Now all we had to do was cross to the other side and we would be home.

'Carmen, *venstre!*' I shouted – the Norwegian word for 'left' – and she immediately turned, pulling the rest of the team with her.

Only the dogs were illuminated by my headlamp. Everything else was a swirl of night and snow that bounced the beam back to me. If I kept going straight, we couldn't miss it. Eventually, we would have to cross the road to reach the yard, but the lights of the coal mine would tell me when to do so. I kept waiting to see its glow from the mountainside, but there was nothing.

We kept going forward until it was impossible to tell what direction we were heading in, or if we were moving at all. It felt as if we were trapped in the belly of something. I looked behind me to make sure two sleds were still following; they were, although I could only see a blurry outline of the second one. In front of us, the same cabin we had passed fifteen minutes ago appeared again. We had gone in a big circle and not realised it.

We tried again. All we had to do was find the road. Carmen started pulling to the right on her own, and I stopped the sled so I could correct her.

'*Gå fram!*' 'Go forward!' She turned to look back at me with a stubborn gaze, as if she were unimpressed, unfazed by this whole situation.

'Come on, Carmen, let's go,' I told her. Still nothing – she wasn't convinced. She kept trying to pull to the right.

Fine. Why not? I let her lead; at some point dogsledding seems to be about trust between the musher and the team, that equal meeting point where you work together and find a trail where there isn't one.

We heard it out of nowhere. Howling, barking. A pack of dogs somewhere in the dark. It was as if they were calling to us. Carmen was leading us toward the sound. She knew! As we came closer, I could see the outline of the coal mine near our kennel. Then the ring of lights from the dog yard, the tiny silhouettes of dogs and their houses. Home was finally in view.

During the ride, I had kept thinking about the conversation I'd had with the guests at our camp the night before. We were discussing all the different reasons a person would want to come up here, to one of the most northern settlements in the world, where there's so much space and contrast in the landscape. A place that's both beautiful and intimidating. They told me they did it to test themselves, to do something completely different from their daily lives in the city.

In a way, I can relate to them with my decision to move north. Even though the Arctic can be harsh with its twenty-four-hour night, its elemental fierceness, there aren't many things that beat the feeling of coasting through those quiet, still days on a dogsled, where it's only the sound of measured breathing and paws pushing through snow. Along with the challenges come rewards, and every time the sun disappears for months, the thought of that first slow sunrise in March is what makes me persevere through winter. And then I think about dogs like Carmen, who taught me how to live fearlessly, how to always keep going towards whatever mystery lies ahead.

Kelsey Camacho lives in Longyearbyen, Svalbard, where she guides nature trips by both dogsled and boat. Her work has appeared in *Proximity* magazine, *Entropy* magazine, the *Portland Review*, and elsewhere.

From *Charles: The Story of a Friendship*

Michael Joseph

Michael Joseph, writer and publisher, wrote Charles: The Story of a Friendship *after his beloved Siamese cat died in 1942. Over the course of thirteen years, they had formed a strong bond, and Charles often sat upon Michael Joseph's desk when he worked at home before the war.*

On the long train journey to Cornwall, Charles was unexpectedly docile. Already he seemed to have made up his mind that he was in safe hands; or it may be that he philosophically accepted the discomforts of travel as an inescapable feature of his new life.

I did what I could to ease the journey for him. The basket had been cleaned out, a fresh strip of blanket had been put in and folded up around the sides to protect him against draughts. I took a saucer and a bottle of milk and a few dry biscuits, for which he had already shown a great liking. There was also a slice of cold grilled sole. 'A present for the leetle cat,' said the amused *maître d'hôtel* when I lunched at his restaurant the previous day.

Best of all, from Charles's point of view, he had room to move about inside the basket, which was big enough for a small dog. (It had in fact been sold to me as a dog basket: I have never liked the tiny hampers which are commonly used as cat baskets.) After I had coaxed Charles into it and shut the wire door he amused himself by thrusting a sturdy pale-brown paw through the wire in a painstaking effort to undo the latch. This being impossible, he contented himself with pushing an inquisitive nose against the wire, eager to see what was happening. All this was accompanied by a clamorous noise which continued all the way to Paddington. But once in the train he settled down to sleep.

In my preoccupation with his welfare I omitted to buy a ticket for him and this led to an amusing incident on the train. When the ticket collector came round, Charles was having an after-lunch sleep on my knee. The ticket collector inspected him with close interest. I hastily mentioned that I had forgotten to buy a ticket for him. The collector thumbed a small book. 'He'd best travel free,' he said. 'Can't find any set charges for marmosets.'

My family were spending their summer holiday at Fowey, a favourite place with us at the time. I had written to them about Charles, giving a full account of his doings, omitting, however, any reference to his disconcerting fierceness. I thought that would be a nice surprise for them.

Charles was not at all embarrassed by the enthusiastic welcome he received. Refreshed by his long hours of sleep in the train he was now wide awake and full of mischief.

He surveyed the furnished house we had taken as though it had always belonged to him. I took the precaution of removing to safety all small breakable objects and some large ones, but Charles was not aggrieved. Polished floors and rugs might have been provided for his exclusive entertainment and he rushed from one corner to another, greatly alarming my wife's mother, who was ill at ease with cats at the best of times. To her Charles, with his unfamiliar appearance and strident voice, was quite terrifying.

'He's more like a young bull than a cat,' she declared. And for a long time afterwards she always referred to Charles as the bull. Charles for his part was cheerfully indifferent to such insults. Some years later my mother-in-law admitted that Charles was the only cat she ever grew to like, and that was one of the greatest compliments ever paid him.

His first visit to the seaside provided Charles with many new experiences, nearly all of them to his liking. There was, for instance, an exciting game with prawns. He soon discovered how to fish live prawns out of a bucket of sea water, and his antics with prawns, shrimps and small fishes collected from rocky pools were most diverting. Having ejected the unfortunate creature by means of a paw gingerly inserted into the bucket, he would prod it into motion all over the balcony which ran in front of the house, prancing after it and all around it, in sheer delight. This pastime would continue until some kind-hearted person came to the rescue of his victim and restored it to the bucket and hence back to the pools where it belonged.

Our summer holidays in those days were very much a family affair. Except for Rupert the canary and the goldfish, who were boarded out, all the animals, even the white mice, accompanied us. Florence Nightingale, who never travelled without her cats – and she had many more than we had – would have approved. The cavalcade of baskets and other animal paraphernalia which passed in procession along railway station platforms must have been impressive, but I was usually too busy presiding over details of the journey to observe the interest we must have aroused in other travellers.

Minna and Peter were old hands at the game and knew what to expect when trunks and suitcases were produced and opened. They viewed all the preparations with alarm. Peter barked his displeasure and Minna showed every sign of agitation, hiding her kittens and generally doing her best to be left behind. But I fancy that it was no more than the nervousness of the bather who thinks the water will be too cold. Once in, all is well; and so it was with our animals. The journey over, they settled down to enjoy their holiday. I may say, in passing, that we never had the slightest fear of any of our cats straying from their holiday homes. They were kept in a quiet room while unpacking was done and after that they were allowed to make the usual thorough inspection of the new house. There may be some truth in the proverbial attachment of cats to houses but our cats at least were attached to us, wherever we were.

On this occasion Charles and I joined the family in the Isle of Wight, arriving late one Friday evening. We had taken a furnished house in Seagrove Bay, which was ideal for a family holiday, as sands and sea were directly in front of the house. It was a pleasant summer evening when Charles and I arrived, and after dinner and Charles's examination of the house, a ceremony no cat neglects, I took him out on to the beach. There was a bright moon and we had the beach to ourselves. At Fowey the year before Charles had only once seen the sea at close quarters and I was curious to see if he remembered that somewhat alarming experience. Whether it was the effect of the moon, which is said to have an influence on cats, or the deserted beach or the quiet mood of the sea I do not know, but something had an immediately intoxicating effect on Charles. He raced all over the sands chasing his shadow, hiding behind rocks and pouncing out on me when I went after him. He ran into the creaming, phosphorescent surf and darted out again. He leapt into the air like an inspired ballet dancer, jumped over the rocks with the grace and agility of a steeplechaser and was not content until I joined him in a breathless game of hide and seek.

Michael Joseph (1897–1958) was born in London. A distinguished publisher, he was also the author of several books on the subjects of writing and cats.

From *Me, My Bike and a Street Dog Called Lucy*

Ishbel Holmes

My eyes shot open into darkness. I didn't dare even the motion of a breath. Lying still in my sleeping bag, I concentrated hard to visualise the scene outside my tent. Male voices, loud and drunken, not far away. The ruttering of an engine. I was well-hidden, camped in a secluded spot surrounded by hedgerows, trees and empty fields. No-one knew I was here.

The men began shouting. Holy shit. They can't be shouting at me! The shouting and jeering got louder. Pretending this wasn't happening I closed my eyes tight. They were not shouting at me. Which was a ridiculous idea because there was no-one else they could be shouting at. I tried to count the number of voices, but there were too many and I realised in that moment: whatever was going to happen, good or bad, was out of my control. So, I lay still and hoped if I ignored the problem it would go away.

Then I thought of Lucy. She was outside. I couldn't hear her. Was she in danger?

I'd been cycling the world for five months, pedalling my way across my tenth country, Turkey, when I met Lucy.

I'd been following a quiet coastal route, looking for a place to camp, when I was greeted with the surprise of a light-coloured dog padding along to the rear of my bicycle. In road racing we were taught to ride in the blind spot of the competitor in front, allowing us to remain hidden whilst conserving energy. This dog was absolutely nailing my blind spot! I smiled, but I knew it was best not to acknowledge or feed random dogs en route. Other cycle tourers had prewarned me, 'Remember, you're cycling the world; stray dogs are not your problem!' Pushing on the pedals I blasted away as only a pure sprinter can, a human machine of fast-twitch muscles designed for power and speed. I glanced behind once more. The dog was running after me as fast as it could, trying to hold its position. I noticed its moving shape was odd, perhaps a limp.

I'd kept on, faster and faster, repeating the mantra, 'I'm cycling the world and stray dogs are not my problem!' A gentle but long downhill was enough to give me the extra speed I needed. The dog fell behind. Another glance to the rear. I could still make out the shape, a small dot way back in the distance. For the love of God, why was it still running? *Give up*, I pleaded silently.

When she was still by my tent the next morning, I cycled slowly back to the nearby village, hoping she would go home. But having cycled across so many foreign countries on my own meant I was highly attuned to my environment and I sensed danger. Then came angry barking from a field on my right and I saw four dogs running across the road. I shouted out, but the dogs reached her and attacked all at once. To my absolute horror the dog lay down. She didn't run. She didn't fight back. She just lay down and accepted what was happening, the dogs snapping with teeth and saliva at her injured hip and leg.

In that moment, I was transported back to being sixteen years old in the back of a car when I didn't fight back. I hadn't cared enough to fight back. For months, I'd lain in bed at night silently screaming. Sometimes punching the pillow, mostly punching myself. I promised to God or the universe or whoever was in charge of the world that I'd be good. Just please give me my family back. But nothing changed.

I was on my own. In foster care. Surrounded by strangers. Because I was such a horrible girl my own family didn't want me. Eventually, I had stopped saying no, grateful finally to be punished. I deserved this.

I threw down my bike and ran screaming towards the dogs with a force I'd never known. Everything happened within seconds as a blur, kicking and pulling the dogs off, still screaming, until they ran away. She was lying on her side. I knelt down, tears filled my eyes. I spoke softly to her that everything was going to be OK. She moved her head just enough to lick my hand. Her big chocolate-brown eyes looked into mine and melted my heart. In that moment, I named her 'Lucy'. She needed my help, just like I had needed help all those years ago. 'You're a good girl,' I said.

I decided then I'd take her to a dog sanctuary where she'd be cared for. The only problem was that it was hundreds of kilometres away. And so I'd stood looking at the already fully loaded bicycle thinking, *Wow, I have to somehow fit a twenty-kilogram dog on there too, and then cycle it.* I walked the bicycle and Lucy to the outskirts of the next town, and stopped at what looked like a hardware store. I motioned to the shop assistant to come over and if charades were a featured discipline in the Olympics, my performance would have been gold medal worthy. The shop assistant returned carrying a thin wooden vegetable crate, metal wire and pliers.

I removed the luggage hanging over my front wheel and strapped it to the sides of the rear bags, then knelt down and began attaching the crate to the front of the bike with wire. Within seconds, my hands were black and my face too from wiping sweat from my brow. Local residents had begun watching the show on their pavement. Word was spreading the box was for the dog. My hands began to bleed from the wire and the oil mixed in with the blood. Finishing, I stood up and wiped my hands on my floral skirt, which was exactly why I'd chosen such a pattern. I touched the crate and it rocked slightly from side to side. Well, this was the best I could do in this moment with what I had. I cushioned the inside of the crate with cycling tops, making sure the red tartan Scottish one was to the top. I knew my dog carrier was a bit wobbly, but I was amazed I had done it all by myself. I stood back looking at the bike, box and Lucy. This was never going to work, but I had no choice.

Now, just two nights and tricky cycling days later, Lucy was outside my tent and I had to protect her. So many people hated dogs in Turkey. What would they do to her?

The men were still shouting at me. I was petrified. I slowly pulled on the zip of the entrance, my face screwing up in panic each time I made a noise; then I paused, not daring to look. But I had to for Lucy. I peeked out just enough to see a tractor with its engine running and lights illuminating the surrounding area. Several men stood jostling around on the trailer behind it, raising beer cans in the air and shouting over to my tent. I couldn't see Lucy.

I had to try something. I shouted as forcefully and alpha-like as I could. 'GO AWAAAAAY!!!'

One voice shouted back, 'Do you want me? Do you want me?' and the others burst out laughing. Oh shit. They began jumping over the side of the trailer and into the field towards my tent. I hoped Lucy had run away and was safe. I begged to no-one in particular, *Please don't let this be happening; please don't let this be happening.*

Then a deep growling filled the air. The men froze, and fell silent. The growling got louder and terrified even me. Lucy's shape appeared in the darkness, moving slowly towards them. *Oh God, please don't do that Lucy.* I didn't want her to get hurt. She stopped in between myself and the men. I got ready because if any one of them got her I would attack with everything I had. Lucy dropped her front legs and head, as though she were getting ready to pounce at the men, and remained in this position growling even louder. The men turned and ran as fast as they could back to their trailer shouting 'Dog, Dog' as the engine powered up, rumbling them away into the darkness.

Lucy remained in position, her ears and nose to the air. I remained still, not making a sound. Lucy relaxed and finally turned around, padding towards me and bowing her head to lick my hand as she reached me. I hugged her with my whole heart. Lucy had protected me. She had saved me. I whispered 'Thank you' over and over.

I invited Lucy inside the tent, but she went back to her place outside. I got back in my sleeping bag, but was unable to sleep. I had backpacked and cycled many countries in my life and this was the first time I had ever felt in danger travelling a country because I was a woman. If this had happened just two days before there would have been no Lucy protecting me. I thought back to Lucy chasing me as hard as she could and I wondered who was rescuing who?

Ishbel Holmes (www.worldbikegirl. com) has cycled twenty countries solo and rescues street animals as she pedals. She advocates for elderly people, is an ambassador for young people and, much to the dismay of  her friends, is an avid wearer of socks and sandals. Follow her adventures across social media at World Bike Girl, and read more in *Me, My Bike and a Street Dog Called Lucy*.

AFRICA

Habibi

Sheelagh Reynolds

The sun had his hat on. Big time. He was shining so hard and hot on to the square in the centre of Chefchaouen that every living thing seemed to have put life on hold for a while. The shopkeepers stopped their hassling, the tourists took a break from their bargaining and the dogs lounged listlessly, sprawled out on the ground under the tables and chairs set outside the numerous cafés. Even the swallows had taken a break from their frantic, swooping, fly-catching activities in favour of hunkering down inside their hole-in-the-wall nests until the heat grew a little more tolerable. I stopped too and sat down under a tree with a glass of sweet, iced mint tea in order to gather my strength for a final round of bantering battle with the wily shopkeepers. Sitting became a slump and shortly thereafter a full horizontal pose.

My friend and I had come to the end of a wonderful Moroccan odyssey that had taken us from the fishing port of Essaouira in the west, up into the High Atlas Mountains in the centre of the country, down again to the souks of Marrakech and Fez and now, in enchanting, pastel-blue-washed Chefchaouen, I was intent on a last-minute gathering of mementos to jigsaw into my luggage. A small rug, an ammonite – definitely; a wrought-iron framed mirror – possibly; a mosaic-topped table – almost certainly not. But not in my wildest dreams had I considered Habibi.

Out of the corner of one half-closed eye, I gradually became aware of movement emanating from a small, dome-shaped object in a cage about twelve inches square set on the cobbles nearby. First one scaly little leg, then another; then two more legs extended very, very slowly out from under a tiny carapace. At the front end an ancient face; at the back a small, pointy tail. A tortoise, an excuse for a tortoise, smaller than the palm of my hand, banged up in solitary in the fearsome heat with no food and no water. 'Help me!' he (or she) was surely crying as he banged into the bars of the cage and opened his mouth to reveal a shiny pink interior. And so I did. I bought him and took him away in a plastic bag.

Back in our hotel Habibi – the name means 'my love' in Arabic – very quickly made himself at home. I had bought provisions – tomatoes, greens, a carrot – while the lid of a nearly empty jar of Nivea sufficed as a water bowl. Habibi immediately tucked in, employing his rather large tongue to get the food into his mouth and making surprisingly loud crunching noises for a creature so diminutive. Having completed his meal he wandered off under the bed, tucked all his bits back inside his shell and proceeded to do a very good impersonation of a pebble.

The next step should probably have been to return Habibi to the surrounding barren hills where he could meet up with his kind and live happily ever after – if not recaptured. But this is not what happened. I had recently buried my old dog and missed him dreadfully. I wanted some animal companionship, someone to welcome me home after a long day at work, and it occurred to me that Habibi might just fit the bill. This would, of course, involve smuggling...

Many years before, as a student, I had done a good bit of smuggling without a second thought and without a shred of nerves. I lived in Jersey where the allowance of duty-free cigarettes to take over to the mainland for each university term was just two hundred. I would carefully remove the outer cellophane from the carton, empty all the cigarettes from their boxes and return them individually to the carton, managing to pack in quite a few more than the original two hundred. The tricky bit was easing the wrapper back over the carton, but the result looked good enough to sail through customs every time.

Travelling from Jersey to Heathrow involved one custom point; this particular journey involved no fewer than five. From Chefchaouen we travelled to the port of Ceuta. Here were two custom points, because although Ceuta is on the African continent, it is in fact Spanish and there is a no-man's-land and rather a lot of armed guards overseeing emigration. Over the water, at Algeciras, lay number three.

Habibi was nonplussed (unlike my friend) and obligingly continued his pebble impersonation in my rucksack. However, and perhaps in the nick of time, it occurred to me that if he were to extrude his six appendages, namely head, tail and four limbs, his image on the X-ray machine might give the game away. And so, at each of the five challenges, I tucked him down the front of my jeans and took him through the metal detector arch with me. Tortoise in pants, heart in mouth.

We spent a night in Algeciras where training began in earnest as there was no money left for a final night out. 'Habibi, come!' Pebble. 'Habibi, fetch.' Pebble. I was beginning to wonder if I may have made a mistake, but there was no going back now. My friend and I played cards, drank our Baileys and had an early night – perchance to dream. Not a chance! All night long the would-be pebble clattered noisily across the bathroom tiles, banging into everything in his path – toilet pedestal, waste bin, shower tray – all the while excreting unreasonable amounts of slimy processed vegetable matter from his rear end.

Habibi seemed to enjoy the flight home and was very active despite his night out on the tiles. I took a photograph of him sitting on the plane seat next to me enjoying the lettuce from my sandwich.

We made it home. I made a pen which took up more than half my not-very-big kitchen. I hired a light to keep him warm. He never greeted me with enthusiasm. Never wagged his tail. Never asked to be let out. 'My love' was a disappointment.

But Habibi went to a far better home. He lived in an incubator for three years until he was big enough to cope with the English climate. I now have two guinea pigs, and still think about getting a dog.

Sheelagh Reynolds was born and brought up in Jersey and lived in Hong Kong and New Zealand for a good part of her adult life. After retiring from a late-onset career in midwifery she embarked on a year of solo travel, and is currently pondering what on earth to do next.

From *The Sky is on Fire*

Magsie Hamilton Little

In the back of an open truck a young dromedary appeared to be floundering. It was frothing at the mouth, its feet were slipping and it was gasping for breath. There was no ramp for it to climb down and no men to lift it, just a small boy. The lad, who cannot have been ten years old, appeared to have forgotten the Koran's instruction to be kind to animals. His stick fell hard on the scrawny rump. Down it came again. And again. And again.

The camel screamed in defiance. There was blood in its mouth and on the rope.

Together we watched, Samir and I, without speaking, as the feeling of helplessness grew worse.

A frantic scrabbling began, toes on the hot, metal flatbed, until in one clumsy movement, the beast toppled earthward. At last it couched, legs folded underneath its deflated body, its head hung low, its long, muscular neck almost on the ground. It did not move.

That was when I cracked.

Half an hour later my travel purse was empty. Dazed and confused, I sat on the sand, the proud new owner of a very sick-looking dromedary. The seller and the crowd had left long ago.

There are some moments in life that are like pivots around which everything turns. A flicker of intuition, a flash of inspiration, and suddenly we know we have made the right decision. I watched the sunlight splash the hump with gold streaks and saw that this was one of them. It was an instant of pure, uncomplicated knowing and it lasted about ten seconds.

The camel opened its eyes. It gazed at me, apparently oblivious to the flies caking its lashes and blackening its head, and then it gurgled delicately.

In that split second I felt myself melt. 'It' became 'she' and I was suddenly in love.

Almost immediately my heart began to sink. It was that feeling when you know you have conned yourself into something even Sisyphus would not have attempted – and there is no going back.

It is all very well setting off for a distant country trying to persuade yourself that you are going to learn something, that you are an independent person and you know what you are doing because you have done it many times before and that everything will work out; but when somehow you find yourself having parted with a large lump of cash, when you are alone with a stranger in a remote corner of the desert, with nothing to go on but a ridiculous act of impulse and a preposterous idea that even you have no faith in, it suddenly seems much more inviting to be sitting in a café in Tuscany, with old friends, sipping a respectable Chianti and reading books about romantic getaways in the desert.

Samir was giving me that 'I *knew* you were mad and because you are from the West *and* a woman what just happened didn't surprise me' look of his.

As he struggled with his preconceptions I ventured, 'I guess we need a name,' more by way of a distraction than anything else.

He scratched his chin, studying her, drinking her in, from her sore feet, her shredded legs and her dull eyes to her limp tail. He retreated into her stillness, as if absorbing her pain.

Suddenly he pulled up his veil. 'Miteuse,' he sighed. It meant 'fleabag'.

I raised my head, horror-struck. 'We can't call her *that*! She's beautiful.' I could not help but adore her long thick lashes, her gungy eyes, her silky ears, her blubbery lips and rotten teeth. There was a nobility about her. I was blind to the ticks, the fleas and the ringworm.

'Do you know any vets?' I said, trying to remain calm.

The Tuareg who had been good enough to drive me around Tamanrasset was lost in thought. 'Perhaps,' said Samir enigmatically, after a long pause.

I was left wondering what exactly he meant by that when a faint whispering began. It was the sizzle of camel feet on sand. Then, with a violent shuffling and jerking she stood up, hovering uncertainly, as if her spindly legs might give way at any moment. Balance came gradually, with more words of encouragement and the last few drops in the water bottle.

Against a pale sky with a new moon floating in it like a silver feather, we rounded the curve of the track to the gentle padding of camel feet.

By a fluke of fate, two major advantages helped to make the project of healing a camel slightly less unworkable than I had imagined. The first was Samir's father, Suleyman, a Tuareg nomad with a penchant for whisky and a soft spot for camels. The second was plain luck.

Tuareg tradition holds that a camel's spirit is just as important as its body. For Fleabag to make a full recovery, psychological and emotional as well as physical, we would need to take her to visit a *marabout*. There was just one tiny snag. He lived miles away, across a scorching plain with no maps and no roads in a region inhabited by known bandits.

While I considered this, day by day, inch by inch, camel hair by camel hair, she grew better. Given the ill treatment of her past, it was unsurprising that she had hated training. As Samir put it, 'Camels always worry about what humans are going to do to them.' The priority was to win her trust, and that meant not asking too much of her at first. Suleyman whispered to her to soothe her nerves, but when he tried loading her, she reared on her haunches and bucked violently. The pack catapulted through the air and landed yards away and when the bucking finally stopped she stood remorsefully, saddled askew on her quivering belly. Only grapes calmed her.

Suleyman groomed her flanks, gently stroking her skinny legs. Some camels have a habitual tendency to kick, and that is dangerous: one strike can break an arm or a rib. Fleabag was a gentler spirit. If irked, she would just vomit cud.

Teaching her to carry a pack was child's play compared to riding her. On his own camel, Samir trotted casually around us, no hands. Having grown up on the sands, as a child he had used no saddle, sitting in front of the hump, leg over the animal's left shoulder. There was nothing you could teach him.

Suleyman barked instructions at me. 'Rest the soles of your feet against her neck so you can feel and guide her. If you want to use the rope, tap the right side of her neck. To run, dig your heels in. To halt, pull.'

I guided, trotted and pressed my heels in. I pulled on the rope. I tapped Fleabag's neck. My veil had unhooked itself and was strangling me, but somehow I managed to cling on.

Gently I patted her neck, clutching my saddle with its small sense of security. That was the moment of disengagement.

The act of falling is never an elegant spectacle. Galileo showed that gravity accelerates all objects at the same rate. He also postulated that air resistance means lighter objects may fall more slowly in an atmosphere. Heavier ones, on the other hand, travel fast.

I brushed myself down and limped to the shade of the palm trees. I took painkillers and got back in the saddle, after which I had difficulty walking unaided.

'It's all about power,' said Suleyman, rather worryingly, 'and submission.' Did he mean the camel or me?

After a few more lessons my wonky vertebrae had rearranged themselves, although for my aching backside there was no respite. Some say that the camel was put upon earth by Allah the Merciful to help the desert people; but in my view it was put upon earth by Allah the Unmerciful to test the endurance of the infidel.

All camels are different and have moods. Sometimes Fleabag's tail swished, at others it hung limp. One moment she seemed proud and stern. The next minute a stomp of irritation took up residence in her face, evident from the nose position. On rare occasions a sense of bonhomie descended and I felt there was hope. At others a hurt, sullen look gave her the appearance of such vulnerability that it became impossible not to hug her.

As soon as I was on her back, she would swing forwards and back again as violently as possible. I would give her an order and she would obey tentatively, navigating the path as if she had heard the instruction and was responding to it. The next time I asked her, she would disobey, and when I showered her with praise she would invariably thank me with fly-filled snot. Like all women, whose prerogative it is to change their mind, sometimes she refused to budge. At others she walked on. She knew where she was going. She remembered the routes.

As the sun turned caramel against the plateau we set off on our usual low-key amble, with long, ungainly strides and an out-of-sync swing – hers or mine, who was to know? Her gait was proud, nose reaching, as if she were registering the scents on the air and determining their origin.

'What's wrong?' Up ahead Samir, on Winaruz, had slowed and we caught up easily.

'Nothing,' I said.

'If you are worrying about visiting the marabout, you should not. If you won't go for yourself, do it for the camel.'

A little way on, where the sand drifts were building, Fleabag halted. Standing motionless, as if struck by a sudden thought, she threw a piercing gaze towards the distant peaks of the Atakor, green-gold against the gloaming sky. The clouds had caught the sunset contours and the wind rippled over the sand like spun silk.

I could just make out the soft drone of the wind and the tempo of my breath, the siren song of the desert. I strained my ears to it.

Fleabag heard it too. She shook her head. Had she arrived at a decision? Did she have a plan? She appeared to understand my doubts and, no sooner than they had been pondered, swung her head to the side. 'I'm not sure who gave you the authority,' that noise said. Then she took off.

We gathered speed before I could register what was happening. My voice tried to steady her, but it felt more anxious than soothing. What was the strange new sensation rising up inside me, the wind on my face, the sun warm against my back? It had been so long coming, this shot of energy, this sudden lightness of being, that I hardly recognised it. I wondered if it might be fun.

I hung on, out of amazement as much as fear, my instinct to cry out, and, as I did so, she answered. 'Roooarrr!' she answered again, an overwhelming, resounding, 'Yes!'

No longer did we lumber. We floated. We knew what to do. We had skills.

So this was it, I thought to myself, as we were flying along. This *was* happiness.

Then, out of the corner of my eye, I caught sight of Samir. No longer was he watching us with his judgemental expression. Winaruz, who was still cantering, joined in with his own triumphant, stomach-splitting bellow. We were four creatures on eight legs thundering across the desert in a moment of oneness.

It felt purely by accident that Fleabag began to slow, and only then on account of the natural flattening off of the slope. Gradually, we settled for a lumpy quickstep, or, as Samir christened it, the 'Saharan bounce', side to side and diagonally.

I pulled the rope and this time, to my surprise, she obeyed. She flicked round her neck and rubbed me. She swished her tail. She swung her haunches.

Just a few days earlier it would hardly have seemed possible, but now Fleabag and I were submitting to each other.

I felt calm, strong, if a little pink and shiny. A new resolve flooded through me. I was ready to take her to the marabout. I didn't care about the risks. I would do it for her.

Magsie Hamilton Little is a writer, academic, charity worker and translator. Her books include *Dancing with Darkness*, *The Thing About Islam* and *The Sky is on Fire*, an account of her time living with Tuareg nomads.

The White Cockerel

Ash Dykes

The streetlights and the Malagasy music gave Bealanana a party atmosphere. Along with an extra guide, Liva, my friend Suzanna was joining us for the final stage of the expedition. We all sat outside at a barbecue place, eating and getting on well. Max and I told them about the previous day's walking and they laughed and said it sounded hideous.

Over four months earlier, I had stood at the southernmost tip of Madagascar, where the Indian Ocean meets the Mozambique Channel, about to set off on a journey that had never been completed before: to walk the entire length of the island, some sixteen hundred miles. My goal was to take on the eight highest mountain summits, as well as the densest jungles. Now I'd reached the final stage, three more mountains to go to the northernmost point.

The first hiccup came the next day at Mangindrano, the last settlement where we'd have the chance to stock up on food. The trouble came with the national park's permit that we'd need to access the final peak, Maromokotro. The officials told us that this entrance to the national park was for research and science purposes only, and that we'd have to go back to Antananarivo and get a stamp and letter of invitation. There were no roads around here and it had taken me and Max a month to walk from there. We weren't going to walk back. We tried everything and then, with no-one able to help, we decided to go for it anyway, and told the officials we wouldn't be entering the national park. I wasn't risking the expedition for a permit.

Before we left, we had one more thing to arrange. The locals said we must take a white cockerel with us to the peak of Maromokotro, to keep the bad spirits away from us in the forest. So we got one, a shy little guy, the only white cockerel available. I like choosing unsuitable names for things on my expeditions, and so I named him 'Gertrude'. It made me laugh just saying it. Gertrude would have to come with us for the next two or three weeks and we'd release him alive on the peak of Maromokotro as a sacrifice. We also had to buy a small bottle of rum and a tub of honey; we would mix the two together on the peak and take a shot, so the bad spirits would allow us back down safely.

I kept Gertrude in my hands – it was too hot for him to go in the top pouch of my rucksack. He was snowy white, about a foot tall when standing straight, but slender and light with very long legs. I knew he'd won three cockfights previously, so he had to be tough, and maybe he'd bring us luck. He seemed healthy, strong and confident, a very chirpy character, always aware of and curious about his surroundings – I called him 'the leader of all chickens'!

It was the rainy season now and the rivers were bigger, the ground marshier. I took the lead, machete in hand, through the bush and dead bamboo, the lemurs howling and leaping about above us in the trees. We hacked through all sorts of dense jungle, from wiry bush that trips you up, gets caught around your ankles and holds you down, to sharp new bamboo spearing up through the ground. In the rainy season, paths get overgrown. We had to keep our distance from the person in front so we weren't hit in the face by branches, watch out for the leeches which dropped from the trees, and take our packs off to tunnel through the bamboo. We pulled our bodies up cliff faces. We battled for hours, but were only a few hundred metres from where we'd woken up that morning. It was amazing when we finally hit Ambohimirahavavy at 2,301 metres: there was nothing to see except mist and thick jungle, with creepers and moss hanging from the branches.

Setting up camp, we kept Gertrude safe on a length of string tied to a tree, and at night he stayed safe on top of my tent. He adjusted well to the daily routine. It was amazing to see that he would never stray too far and whilst pecking at the floor for any bugs he could find, he would occasionally lift his head to check we were still in sight. On the rainy days he wouldn't run from me when it was time to sit him in the top compartment, almost as if he looked forward to it. But on hot days we had to take breaks often to let him get some air and cool off.

We were in the jungle for three days and covered just seven miles trying to reach the next mountain. We couldn't go on like this – it would take us weeks and we'd run out of food. The only option was to go back the way we'd come. If we went back to Mangindrano we could top up on food, reassess our route and maybe find a guide. Waterproofs on, we trekked back up the mountain, stopping over and over to pull off leeches which were washed off the trees by the rain and fell down our tops. Suzanna's waterproof poncho seemed to attract more leeches than anything else and she was covered in them, inside and out, her face bleeding too. Liva and Max were wearing shorts so their legs were dripping blood. After a very steep trek for a few hours, we made it back to the old camp spot. Somehow, despite everything, we were still all in high spirits, looking forward to recharging our batteries and finding someone who knew the way. Even Gertrude seemed happy sticking with us. He needed us and we needed him.

We went back to our old corner of the village, then to the lady who made banana fritters. We hung our kit over the bamboo fences as the late afternoon sun came out from behind the clouds, washed in the river and laughed about the adventure of the last few days. By this time Gertrude had become domesticated and wouldn't leave us alone. We left him at the back of the house with the other chickens, but he found a way through to the bedroom and jumped on the windowsill to be next to us, looking down at us curiously, his head cocked, out of one eye then the other. He spent the night here, and seemed to be looking forward to coming with us up more mountains.

The jungle had chewed us up and spat us out, but we were heading back for more. We figured out a new route, and I was excited as we set out. The mountain passes were beautiful but the cliffs steep and dangerous in places. At a tiny village we stopped to cook noodles. I managed to burn myself and spilt half my bowl on the floor. Gertrude ate it for me, then chickens started to gather. Gertrude chased them off and attacked one of the others. I held him back and broke it up.

The villagers were busy crushing rice when we woke up early to a hot sun and blue sky. As we climbed, the heat was intense. We took river breaks so Gertrude could drink water and cool down. There were times when having Gertrude around made things worse – when I was hot, hungry, tired, thirsty and frustrated, he'd be constantly making noises, annoying cockerel noises right at the back of my head. I was finding it tough and had zero energy after the ordeals of the previous months. But there were also times when Gertrude would lift our spirits. As I walked, I'd occasionally laugh out loud at the fact I was carrying a cockerel in my backpack – and it seemed normal.

The final goal, Gertrude's goal (although he didn't know it), was Maromokotro. Locals warned us about the big rivers. The first wasn't too deep, but the current was strong and we worked as a team to help each other across, balancing the bags on our heads. Lemurs swarmed our camp one morning. We waved tree branches in front of our faces to battle the tiny flies that constantly aimed for our eyes, noses, ears and mouths. My trainers had been soaked through for days, and sand inside was rubbing my feet raw. I borrowed Liva's flip-flops, three sizes too big, to tackle the beautiful mountain which now appeared before us.

We ditched the bags and placed a waterproof cover over them for the last section, taking just my satellite phone, Gertrude, the rum and honey. We were all soon soaked through and the walk seemed to go on forever. We had estimated two hours, but it took four, as the path had grown over and the lads were slightly lost. I had Gertrude in my arms and when it started raining, he hated it and tried escaping; I had to grip tight and keep hold of him until the summit.

When we eventually made it, we were freezing so we had no patience to linger. I tucked Gertrude under some rocks away from the rain, as he was freezing also. I wanted to take him to the next village, but I knew that would be going against the local traditions. Part of me hoped that he would casually follow us down off the mountain, but he was tired, cold and wet and just wanted to stay under the rocks, protected from the elements. It didn't feel right – he was a member of the team, had been a part of the journey – but I had known this time would come. He was a survivor, the toughest of cockerels, and I believe he is still up there, not only surviving, but thriving.

It was done: I had successfully summited the highest mountain in Madagascar (and the other seven highest), even though we hadn't got that official piece of paper. It felt bloody good. But I'm sure I couldn't have done it without Gertrude.

Ash Dykes was born in Wales. By the age of twenty-five he had become the first person to walk solo and unsupported across Mongolia, and the first to traverse Madagascar via its eight highest peaks. The story  above was adapted from his first book, *Mission Possible: A Decade of Living Dangerously*.

Painted Wolves

Jonathan Scott

In the 1980s, my lifelong obsession with the highly social (pack-hunting) African wild dog took me into the Serengeti National Park in Tanzania where I lived alone in my safari vehicle for weeks at a time, immersing myself in the life of the pack. It was a never-to-be-forgotten experience, culminating in the book, Painted Wolves: Wild Dogs of the Serengeti-Mara *(1991). During that period, I learned as much about myself as I did these extraordinary social hunters, who sadly number just a few thousand animals throughout Africa due to loss of habitat and conflict with livestock owners. The following is an extract from my autobiography,* The Big Cat Man *(Bradt Travel Guides, 2016).*

The highlight of my time during those years in Serengeti was when the Ndoha pack denned at Handajega, deep in the Western Corridor, in May 1987. No tourists visited Handajega in those days. I had never known solitude like this before, never felt so totally isolated from everything that previously had made me feel human – the sense of quiet in my brain was palpable. Surrounded by a landscape of palm-fringed watercourses and dense thickets opening into wide open spaces, I was able to immerse myself in the life of the pack. It was just me and the dogs – dogs that I did not know well and that would take time to settle to my presence. I needed to start with a clean slate, to identify individuals, become one of the pack while I waited for the magical moment when the puppies first emerged from the den.

When I arrived, the alpha female immediately started to move her month-old pups to a new den close to the original burrow, carrying them one by one in her mouth. There were twelve in all. I retreated, watching through binoculars to sense the pack's mood, and soon enough some of the adults came trotting over to my vehicle to investigate. Within a day or so they began peeing against the tyres, sniffing the underbelly of the car and ferreting out any loose wires, latching on to anything that they could bite or chew. The whole vehicle would rock as the dogs braced their back legs and leaned into the task, clamping their powerful jaws firmly on to the canvas covering my winch and high-lift jack, yanking and tugging until they shredded it or got bored. Meanwhile I would be brewing up the first cup of tea of the day on my gas cooker.

The wild dogs' greeting ceremony was always one of my favourite moments of the morning and evening, the time when the ragtag assortment of individuals was transformed into a single entity – the pack. Each of these dogs was an individual, its destiny dictated to a large degree by its own nature: some equal, some subordinate, some top of the hierarchy as alpha male or female, some destined always to follow and never to breed. But what I found so fascinating was that each of them was also a vital part of something larger than themselves. Wild dogs on their own struggle to survive, but as part of a pack they take on a collective power, intelligence and energy that is wonderful to behold.

Waiting for the dogs to stir towards the end of the day was like being with a pride of lions or a leopard as the heat of the sun dissipated and a gentle breeze swept towards them. The dogs would stretch out their long slender legs and yawn, each gently jolted from its slumber by the same silent wake-up call coursing through their veins. While a leopard might sit and contemplate its next move or a lion get up and then flop down again alongside a fellow pride member until the light had faded from the sky, the dogs would rise and run around. They greeted their own-age mates, responding to subtle nuances of body language, ears either cocked or laidback, eyes staring or downcast. Then as a subgroup they would run to younger or older dogs, brothers or sisters, parents or uncles and aunts, yearlings or puppies who would already be going through the same ritual with their own-age mates, uttering high-pitched wittering calls like hungry pups, licking into each other's mouths, peeing and crapping with unbridled excitement. If they were hungry, and they generally were – they often hunted morning and evening when they had pups – they would trot off in single file into the thickets in search of impalas, or out on to the plains in pursuit of the fleet-footed Thomson's gazelles. And if there were wildebeest in the area they would search for the young calves that were the mainstay of their hunting forays at this time of year.

I would follow in their wake so as not to disturb them unduly, the tail-end Charlie of the pack. If I tarried a while a dog might run back towards my vehicle, almost as if to see if I was joining them or not. When the dogs spotted suitable prey they slowed to a walk, bunching up shoulder to shoulder, their large bat ears cocked with intent and anticipation, then folded back to reduce their silhouette as they stalked as close to their quarry as possible. You could feel the tension rippling through their lean frames, every muscle and sinew gathering for the charge forward that I knew was coming.

The minute the wildebeest or gazelles turned and began to flee, the dogs would be after them like a pack of hounds hunting a hare or stag, racing flat out to close the distance on the animal they had targeted, constantly watching for signs of weakness or disadvantage – an injury to a leg or a disease such as mange. They homed in on the young and vulnerable, old and infirm, with the pack sometimes splitting up to hunt more than one animal when they were particularly hungry or had a lot of mouths to feed. All the while I could feel my own heart rate rising, the adrenaline coursing through my veins with the excitement of the chase. Emotionally I was always with the pack, never the prey, feeling the hunter stirring deep within me.

The dogs would gallop along for kilometre after kilometre until their prey tired sufficiently for them to pull it to a halt or they realised that they had been outrun or outmanoeuvred. It was like watching great athletes: the dogs are long-distance runners with the kick of a sprinter. A hunt always seemed to have a touch of joyful abandon to it, as if they were straining at the leash to be off, long pink tongues lolling out of the sides of their mouths, revelling in the chase and the prospect of food. But there was also a sense of utter determination, an urgency to keep on going until the prey began to weary. Then it was just a matter of time and sometimes the end came mercifully quickly.

Occasionally on a moonlit night the dogs would hunt when the wildebeest herds tarried close by. I would hear the pounding of hoofs, the herds coughing and spluttering in the dust, and the occasional high-pitched yipping of the dogs. The commotion often brought hyenas at the double to try to steal any kill the dogs had made. A hyena might linger, nonchalantly chewing on the metal valve of one of my tyres, prompting me to open the window to tell it to 'bugger off'. Woken from a deep sleep one night by the incessant rocking of the vehicle, I eventually shot out of bed, scrambling over the seat and through the door, yelling at the top of my voice as I sprinted naked across the plains in pursuit of the startled hyena. I then managed to trip over the entrance to a warthog burrow and pitched head first to the ground. Not a pretty sight, but it seemed to do the trick – for a while at least.

Jonathan Scott has lived in Kenya for the past forty years and is married to wildlife photographer Angela Scott. They are the only couple to have won the overall award in the prestigious Wildlife Photographer of the Year competition as individuals. With  a second home at Governors' Camp in the Maasai Mara National Reserve, they have between them produced over thirty books, including Bradt's *A Leopard's Tale* and *The Big Cat Man*. Their latest TV series is the five-part *Big Cat Legacy*. For more see: www.jonathanangelascott.com.

Annie's Story

Richard Kitzinger

It's horrific.

The clearing is a bloodbath.

It's an image that will stay with me for the rest of my life. An elephant on its side with most of its face missing. Just dug away. For its tusks. This great beast has given its life up for the sake of its tusks. Murdered and butchered for eighty pounds of ivory.

I am on a safari game drive. Well, I was. What we have just encountered has put an end to any wildlife spotting. The mood has changed entirely. Neither I nor any of the other three travellers with me in the jeep has any thirst for seeing anything more. The enduring image from this trip will only ever be the appalling scene of slaughter just metres from our vehicle.

Our driver is clearly on edge. He and our guide are jabbering away in a language I do not speak. His body language is enough to tell me that he is not comfortable being at the scene of this crime. It occurs to me that the poachers may not be far away. We can see that they are armed and we know that they lack scruples. It would surely be safest for us to get out of here as quickly as possible.

Our guide, Gideon, kneels next to the elephant's corpse. It's not been dead for long. He calls out to the driver who gets on to the radio. He's reporting the discovery when, suddenly, everyone stops. Something is moving in the bushes at the edge of the clearing. Gideon is out of the vehicle and unarmed. Slowly, very slowly, he retreats on hands and knees, all the time facing the bushes where we saw the movement.

Gideon is nearly within reach of the jeep's doorstep when a tiny trunk pokes through the foliage and lets rip with a trumpet. It's shrill and sounds like an old teacher of mine who used to blow her nose noisily into a handkerchief she then tucked back into the sleeve of her pullover.

In different circumstances it would have been comical, but it's clear what this is. Not only have we chanced upon a freshly poached elephant carcass, but we've also found her orphan.

Nervously the poor little thing emerges into the light. Little thing is right – she's not even a metre tall. Ears flapping, tiny tail swatting flies away, she shuffles forward. Heavens. What she must have just witnessed. She must be in shock, traumatised.

I've never felt so helpless. Gideon and the driver talk some more and then make an urgent couple of calls over the radio. Looking at the baby elephant as it tenderly prods at its dead mother is heartbreaking. There's nothing I can contribute to this situation. I try and focus on something else, try to count the odd fruit of a sausage tree at the clearing's edge.

Gideon appears at the flap between the jeep's cab and the passenger seats. He's received instructions over the radio and he is to stay with the baby elephant while the driver takes us back to camp. We will fetch the open-topped trailer and we'll try to get the little elephant to the ranger station at the entrance to the reserve. Gideon is very apologetic. It means the end of our safari drive, half a day early. There isn't one of us who cares. We all realise that for little Annie, the orphaned elephant, there is now a race against time to get her to somewhere where she can be cared for.

The tracks are rutted and we will all bear bruises on our backsides for days to come. It doesn't matter. The driver rushes us back to the camp and we strike it – tents, folding camp beds, suitcases, kitchen table, chairs, food and all – as fast as we can. It's a good thing the safari is not a sellout. The luggage will all go in the jeep with us so that little Annie can go in the trailer.

Brave Gideon has established some rapport with Annie by the time we return. She is tentatively exploring his features with her trunk whilst he gives her loving pats. He cannot, however, give her any milk and she will need some sustenance if she is to survive. We all form a funnel and cajole the frightened calf towards the trailer and up the ramp. It's far from straightforward. We're asking her to do something that even at her age – Gideon estimates that Annie can be no more than three months old – is instinctively unnatural to her.

Why should she trust us? Before we found Annie the last humans she encountered had killed and maimed her mother who is still prostrate within reach of us. Yet she must sense the kindness in our purpose and gradually she advances up the ramp. Whilst Gideon coaxes her forward from her left side, I am on her right and, with a hand on the wrinkly folds of her hind leg, I try to exert some pressure. It's as much use as if I were to try and push a whole rugby scrum on my own. Annie is little by elephant standards, but she is already seriously heavy.

It seems as though it takes an eternity to get her into the trailer, but finally she is in and Gideon with her. In the jeep we have bags and tents on our laps and stuffed into every possible nook and cranny. For about two hours we drive on dust tracks towards the edge of the game reserve. It's uncomfortable, but there's a greater cause at stake here and it really is a matter of life or death for Annie. Gideon is doing his best to keep the little elephant's spirits up, but she has had a heck of a day already.

Annie is a poppet. She's so young and she is starting to struggle. I see her trunk exploring Gideon's T-shirt front. Can it be that she is seeking out nipples? We need to get her something to drink and soon.

Eventually we reach the ranger station at the park entrance. They have milk there and Annie welcomes it. Gideon informs us that the milk has been laced with some medication to help her to travel and to calm her. He assures us that vets from the elephant orphanage on the edge of the city are in radio contact and are awaiting Annie. That's where we're headed. It's too difficult to try and move her from the trailer. Time is of the essence. She has the milk and water she wants and we get underway again.

Our itinerary has gone out the window, but it doesn't matter. We are all caught up in the drama. None of us can bear the idea of Annie not making it to the elephant orphanage where she will have sanctuary and the care she needs from experts.

As we drive on, picking up a tarmac road some three quarters of an hour after leaving the park, I watch Gideon and Annie. Our guide is kindness personified. He must be in agony sitting in the cramped metal trailer with a frightened baby elephant, but he bears it manfully, smiling reassuringly and murmuring soothing sounds into the little beast's neck. We are going as fast as we can, but the weight of an elephant in the back is something of a hindrance. There's a maxim that slow and steady wins the race. I think we all privately say some prayers that there is truth in that for Annie's sake.

Every now and then the road passes a village. Children come running at the sound of a vehicle on the road, waving their arms and shouting to us, though none of us has a clue what they are saying.

Usually the coolest kids will try to race the jeep for a moment or two. When they see through the bars of the trailer that there's an elephant on board most of them stop, astonished. It's not a sight they witness every day of the week.

There's not a moment to waste, however. We have to deliver the little thing to her saviours. Every now and then she lets fly with a trumpet, but the volleys are becoming feebler to the point of being pitiful. It's awful watching, powerless, as Annie fades. She and Gideon are absolutely covered in dust which must be making the pair of them extremely thirsty.

Our fabulous driver swings the jeep and trailer between the gates of the elephant orphanage, a primed guard on the gates lifting the barrier as he sees us approaching. The engine hasn't even been cut before keepers and vets from the sanctuary are opening the trailer and examining Annie. She is weak, but they are confident she has a chance of surviving. It may be more a question of whether she is emotionally prepared to cope without her mother. She will have to put her trust in humans if she is to live and our actions – and particularly the efforts of Gideon – will have helped her to begin to find that confidence in mankind.

There are fourteen other orphaned elephants at the sanctuary, all aged four years and younger. If she makes it Annie will be in good company. She will not want for playmates. The next twenty-four hours will be crucial to her story. For now, though, our part is done and we must say goodbye. We all pat and rub her. Gideon buries his head in her neck. He has developed a bond with the baby elephant. Annie is taken away to receive the nourishment and care she needs and we turn our attention to much more mundane tasks.

Gideon is unashamedly tearful as we fill the trailer with tents, camp equipment and luggage. The man is an absolute hero. If Annie lives it will be because he risked his life to be with her. Whilst we were gone fetching the trailer he was vulnerable to attack from poachers or any number of predatory animals. Had Annie's herd come back they would have trampled him underfoot. He was utterly selfless and deserves a medal. His emotions now spill over and as a group we need to look after him.

We take Gideon and the driver for dinner. Whilst we are at the restaurant we are joined by one of the vets from the elephant orphanage. Annie is doing well and, for the rest of the week before our trip ends, we continue to receive updates on her progress. She is feeling stronger and has already made friends with two other orphaned little girl calves. It's a sad story. Poaching is disgusting and needs to be eradicated. Yet this is a sad story with a great deal of hope in the end.

I still think of Annie and hope that she is happy and healthy.

From echidnas in Tasmania to quetzals in Costa Rica, wildlife has long inspired **Richard Kitzinger** to travel. A freelance writer, he blogs at www.aroundtheworldin18days. uk, accepts commissions to create  bespoke travel plans and has co-written a primary school education pack about red squirrel conservation: www. redsquirreleducation.com.

An Elephant Called Abu

Brian Jackman

Botswana's Okavango Delta is one of the loveliest big game sanctuaries on earth, a miraculous oasis whose marshy spillways and winding channels fan out for more than 15,000 square kilometres across the northern Kalahari. And in the midst of it all is Abu Camp, a luxurious springboard for the ultimate African adventure.

Abu was an African elephant, a majestic bull in his prime who died of a heart attack in December 2002 after fighting with a wild tusker. But two years earlier, for five never-to-be-forgotten days, I rode, walked and swam with Abu and his herd, rocking through the reed beds on his broad grey back, feeling his huge spine flexing beneath me as we splashed across the delta's floodplains on a slow march through paradise.

African elephants are supposed to be untameable: treacherous, unpredictable, not to be trusted. But Randall Jay Moore, a cigar-toting American biologist, former animal trainer and Vietnam War protester, turned convention on its head by offering elephant-back safaris in Botswana.

With Abu were ten other elephants – including Cathy, the herd matriarch – ranging in age from forty-one-year-old, flop-eared Benny to baby Kitimetse, whose Setswana name means 'I'm lost'.

In its heyday Abu's was the most expensive camp in Africa, but guests loved it. One German couple that had met on safari returned for an elephant-back wedding, with the bride seated on Cathy, the groom on Abu and the priest officiating from Benny.

Every morning at first light, my fellow guests and I would be poled by *mokoro*, the traditional Okavango canoe, across the short distance between our camp and the elephants' living quarters. There, at the command 'Stretch down!' Abu and his companions would lower their bodies so that we could clamber aboard. Then Big Joe, the leading mahout, would kick-start Abu with a nudge of his toes behind each giant ear, urging him forward with a cry of 'Move out!' and off we would march in a trunk-to-tail convoy, with little Kitimetse hurrying to keep up at the rear.

Travelling by elephant, I discovered, is the ideal way to explore these languid African 'Everglades'. Bulldozing his way through the tasselled reeds, padding across the Kalahari sandveld or wading belly-deep through oxbow lagoons, Abu was in his element, a perfect, five-ton, all-terrain safari vehicle of awesome power, thoroughly eco-friendly and, apart from occasional bouts of flatulence, entirely pollution-free.

For me this was the greatest safari of my life. Released from the tyranny of roads, you can go where you please, moving soundlessly into the shade of riparian forests, crossing watercourses, eating up the distance at a tireless five kilometres per hour. Furthermore, lounging like a rajah in a padded howdah gives you a new perspective on the bush. Looking down into the amber floodwaters three metres below I could see quick darting bream and tiny frogs like Fabergé jewels clinging to the reed stems.

Game was scarce, having dispersed after the rains. On previous trips clients had seen lion, leopard – even wild dogs. Now only red lechwe antelope remained, plunging like porpoises across the lagoons in a welter of spray. But I didn't care. For once the presence of wild animals seemed almost superfluous. The main attraction was, overwhelmingly, being with Abu and his companions.

By then Abu was probably the world's most famous elephant, having appeared in several movies and co-starred with Clint Eastwood in *White Hunter, Black Heart.*

He was born in the wild in 1960, but then captured and transported to the United States, where he grew up in a Texas safari park, and that is where Randall found him, chained in a barn, smothered in his own dung, sleeping on a bare concrete floor.

On an impulse, Randall bought him for ten thousand American dollars. 'It was,' he said, 'the best deal I ever made.' It was also the beginning of an extraordinary partnership that would ultimately lead them both to a new life in Botswana.

With them came Benny and Cathy, and it was these three riding elephants that became the nucleus of Abu's herd, soon to be joined by what Randall called his 'brat pack' – seven adorable orphaned babies from South Africa's Kruger National Park – and little Kitimetse, the only true-born Botswanan elephant, found abandoned near the camp.

The camp itself was typical of Botswana's low-density, high-price approach to ecotourism, with room for just twelve guests in en-suite tents, where Randall had hosted plenty of celebrities including princes William and Harry. It was here, relaxing in the shade of the mangosteens, that I listened to Randall speaking of his feelings for elephants.

'They're a lot smarter than a lot of people I've met,' he said. 'They can understand more than sixty commands and I can honestly say I generally prefer elephants to people because they never let you down.'

'Their social structure is so like ours in so many ways,' he continued. 'They love their young, become teenagers just as we do, grow old at the same age as us and grieve for their dead. All the best qualities we have as humans I see every day in my elephants.'

I asked him what was the most amazing thing about elephants. 'Look,' he said. 'I'm not a big guy and elephants are very large animals. One hammer blow with their trunk and I'm a goner. They are also so intelligent, and yet there's this relationship where they allow us to dominate them. It's crazy!'

Life at Abu's Camp followed an easy rhythm. Up at dawn for a three-hour ride, followed by lunch and a siesta before heading out again in mid-afternoon. Every ride followed a different route, exploring islands marooned in the floodplains or padding across the Kalahari sandveld.

Out in the drowning seas of grass, Abu's herd became a flotilla, ears flapping like the sails of old-time barges as we rolled on towards the wide horizon. From time to time the elephants would pause to snatch up a trunkful of palm fronds – a take-away snack to be devoured en route. 'Get it and go!' cried the mahouts, and on we rode, with Abu rumbling a message to Cathy and Kitimetse's fat little body outlined in a halo of ginger hairs.

One morning we stopped for a barbecue lunch on an island of ebony trees deep in the delta, where a table awaited us, decorated with jugs of water lilies, and blankets and cushions were spread out in the shade.

Sometimes, instead of riding, I would walk with Sandor Carter, Randall's camp manager. Sandor, a former British Army officer, always carried a rifle in case of emergencies, but never had cause to use it. And it was then, following Abu's giant footsteps through a backlit haze of golden grass-heads, that I sensed what it might feel like to be an elephant. Surrounded by a forest of pillared legs and flapping ears,

I had been admitted into the herd, an honorary member of a close-knit family bound by kinship ties as complex as our own.

Looking up into Abu's benign brown eyes with their long dark lashes, I felt humbled by their tolerance. There was something almost spiritual about being accepted into their company, and to walk with them was to come tantalisingly close to bridging the gap that separates us from the rest of the animal world.

But the high point of the whole safari was the day I swam with Abu in a deep lagoon shared with two bemused hippos and a crocodile, all of whom kept a respectful distance as Sandor, Big Joe and I rode bareback into the water and then submerged on Abu's back, clinging to the tops of his ears as he sank like a submarine beneath us.

When at last it was time to leave I found it hard to say goodbye. When I shook hands with the mahouts I was close to tears, and closer still when I made my farewells with the elephants. I remembered little Kitimetse plucking water lilies as she splashed through the floods, kicking up water like a kid in a paddling pool. I thought of ugly, lovable Benny with his sad eyes and floppy ear, and of course, most of all I missed Abu, the wise and gentle giant who had picked up my lens cap when it fell into the lagoon and handed it back to me in the curled tip of his trunk. Even now, so many years later, I miss them more than I can say.

Brian Jackman is an award-winning freelance journalist and author with a lifelong passion for travel and wildlife. For twenty years he worked for *The Sunday Times*, and was voted Travel Writer of
the Year in 1982. Today his work appears mostly in *The Daily Telegraph*, *BBC Wildlife* magazine, *Travel Africa* and *Condé Nast Traveller*. Although his travels have taken him around the world, he is best known as Britain's foremost writer on African wildlife safaris. His books include *Roaring at the Dawn*, *The Marsh Lions* and *The Big Cat Diary* (both with Jonathan Scott), *Savannah Diaries* and, most recently, *Wild About Britain*, chosen by *The Guardian* as one of the best nature books of 2017.

Follow the Leader

Suzy Pope

Dunes the colour of turmeric made up the Erg Chebbi area of the Moroccan Sahara. I was ready to ride my camel into the middle of nowhere, stand on top of a sand dune and stare out at the neverending desert like a model in an avant-garde watch advert.

The camels smelled like sour milk and mulch, the two of them tethered together like ships in a harbour. Their humps were laden with woven blankets – magenta, fiery red and emerald-green fabric stitched together – while golden tassels and silver bells hung from the wooden saddle frame. The camels should have looked proud, adorned in such splendour, but they sat chewing cud in a slow, circular motion, totally indifferent.

Muhammad, a teenage boy in a yellow turban and robes the deep blue of twilight, was our guide. He led my brother, Alex, to the first camel. Muhammad chattered away while Alex hid behind an unruly fringe, only offering the occasional grunt to his questions. The camel didn't flinch as Alex settled his weight on top of its hump. Muhammad clicked his teeth like an insect and the camel lurched forward before rising to its feet. Our guide stroked the camel's neck and cooed in Arabic.

'This is your camel, miss,' he said, gesturing to the smaller of the two.

As I got closer, its swollen belly gurgled. The camel looked at me and let out a burp so pungent it made my eyes water.

'Nice to meet you, too,' I said.

I placed myself carefully on top of the hump, but as soon as I shifted my weight to get comfortable, a bray rumbled through my camel's body.

'Is it OK?' I asked Muhammad.

'He does not like women,' he laughed.

Great. I had booked a desert trek to get away from society, social media and silent judgement. Now I was stuck for three days with a grumpy, sexist camel.

Muhammad clicked and hissed at my camel, but it wouldn't budge. He got out a short stick and prodded the camel in the side until it rose up like a sullen teenager getting out of bed. My whole body was thrown forward and the metal handlebar caught me in my ribs. I squawked in pain. Maybe if I got to know my camel better it would start to like me.

'What's its name?' I asked Muhammad.

'He is Number Seven, miss,' he replied. 'His brother is Number One. Number One is like BMW of the Sahara.'

His brother is number one. I felt a stab of empathy with Number Seven.

For five days in Marrakech tour guides, shopkeepers and waiters had directed their questions to Alex. I was more talkative, and smiley, but that didn't make a difference.

At the edge of the desert, mounds scattered with plastic bags and cola bottles looked more like builder's sand, as if the Sahara were under renovation. Number Seven rolled from side to side like a boat over waves. It felt like I would slide sideways at any moment so I clung to the handlebar, knuckles white.

Number One kept going, dragging my protesting beast behind. White sand turned orange and dunes swept up to the sky. Every time we passed a date palm or acacia tree, Number Seven would let out a cry of hunger and try to stop. Maybe we had more in common than I thought.

On the twelve-hour car journey from Marrakech Alex had sat in the front. He didn't complain about the long journey or need to stop every couple of hours for another snack. He didn't get restless legs or notice the fizz of lactic acid building up in his knees. He probably could have lasted the whole journey without stopping. I needed to get out and walk about. I got bored in the back seat, and hungry.

The silence became heavier, sounds lost deep in the dunes. My thighs ached and I kept shifting in my seat, trying to get comfortable. Alex leant back like a cowboy, as though he'd been riding a camel for years.

We approached the camp, a cluster of brown tents, as the first stars pricked the sky. Silhouettes of robed men sauntered between dwellings. Smoke rose from a glowing fire.

Muhammad clicked and Number One dropped to the ground, as if kneeling before a sultan. Alex dismounted from his camel and gave it a pat on the head. Number One closed his eyes, content.

It took several clicks, prods and harsh words in Arabic to get Number Seven to kneel. I moved to touch his neck, but he curled his lips, revealing crooked teeth, and snapped at my hand. Muhammad hissed his disapproval.

After a dinner of spiced chicken and couscous I crawled on to a sandy mattress, drifting into the fog of sleep. The ground moved up and down as if I were still riding Number Seven. I heard my camel snicker like a dirty old man, piercing the silence. I snapped awake. My legs ached, and shifting under itchy Berber blankets sent pain through my hips. Number Seven had won this round.

The sun rose, drenching the peaks of dunes in silver light, shadows pooled in the spaces in between. Voices drifted from the specks of people at a camp on the next dune and I could make out distinctly English vowel sounds, laughter and the click and whirr of cameras. So much for isolation and escape. Two elongated black camels stretched across the sand as the sun illuminated Number One and Number Seven. Of course, Number One was sitting patiently waiting for his passenger, while Number Seven had stood up as if to say, 'Right, I'm bored, I'm off.'

As we began the slow plod further into the desert the wind picked up, whipping the side of dunes, throwing sheets of sand across towards Algeria. Muhammad made us stop to wrap scarves around our faces. Number Seven plodded on, long lashes protecting his eyes from the storm.

I'd never been jealous of a camel before.

We stopped by the biggest sweep of dune we'd seen.

'Here is Everest of Erg Chebbi,' Muhammad said. He scratched about in the sand, uncovering what looked like an old tea tray.

'Who wants to go sledging?' he grinned.

The loose end of my scarf streaked behind me like a flag as I scrabbled up the side of the drift. Alex's scarf was a neat bundle around his face. With each footstep my legs sank deeper into the sand. I felt a flicker of respect for Number Seven, plodding his way up these slopes without flinching, every day. No wonder he was always hungry and frustrated.

Halfway up, when it felt like I was slipping back more than I was going forward, I gave up and sat on the tea tray. It glided to the bottom at a pathetic pace, stopping just beside Number Seven who looked unimpressed.

As Alex and Muhammad raced down the dune, whooping and squealing, Number Seven and I both looked on, sulking. They ran up the dune for a second go and I cowered from the wind behind my camel who burped softly away from me. I called it progress.

We arrived at the second camp mid-afternoon. It only took a few clicks from Muhammad to get Number Seven to sit down.

Berber people emerged from tents with trays of sweets and mint tea. I gulped it down, letting the liquid soothe my dry throat. The wind howled and the Berber tents inflated like parachutes with each gust, as though they could take off at any moment.

Darkness cloaked the desert as I scrambled up the side of a dune. Ahead of me Alex strode up, hands practically in his pockets, and sat at the top, staring out at the Sahara like an outdoor clothing model. I slumped down beside him. Whorls of stars and misty galaxies curved across a black canvas. Pulsing drums and wailing song drifted up from around the fire below, distorted on the breeze like a cassette player running out of batteries. Alex shifted on the ridge next to me.

'My arse hurts,' he said. 'I think my camel keeps trying to unsaddle me. It's got some kind of vendetta.'

I could just make out the shape of two camels below, exposed to the elements.

'I hope they're OK out in the storm tonight,' I said.

'It's what they're built for,' Alex said. 'Man, wouldn't it be much better if we could just get a four-by-four out here. Air conditioning, music, comfy seats.'

I was quite enjoying the desert wind, Berber drums and my feet buried in the warm sand like a dry footbath.

'I can't wait to shower and wash the camel smell off,' Alex said.

Maybe I was winning today's camel race.

After Muhammad's wailing dawn wake-up call, I stumbled from my tent, half expecting the camp to have blown away in the night. The dunes were still as a photograph. The camels were already awake, eyes glinting black as beetle shells. Number Seven's jaw rolled as he chewed. I wondered where he'd found something to eat in the middle of nowhere.

I'd either got used to the roll and jerk of Number Seven's awkward gait, or my thighs had become so numb that I couldn't feel the discomfort any more. Ahead of me Alex kept wriggling in his saddle. The dunes seemed endless, as if someone were playing the same film reel over and over. Without the pain in my legs or the wind in my face my mind wandered out into the universe and back again. The only thing marking time was the punch and fade of camel footsteps in the sand.

By mid-morning the sun beat above us. Number One started groaning, breathing air out of his nostrils as violently as a dragon. Muhammad clicked and murmured in Arabic, but Number One stopped and folded himself into sitting position. Alex squawked as the handlebar caught him in the ribs on the way down.

Muhammad gestured for us to dismount while he untied Number Seven and moved him to the front of our tiny caravan.

'See, it hates me,' Alex said, glaring at Number One as we sat with our feet in the sand.

I smiled. Number Seven was in the lead now.

When the small town of Merzouga came into view, Alex breathed a sigh of relief to see the vehicles waiting to whizz us back to the land of flushing toilets and hot showers.

I patted Number Seven on the side to show my appreciation. His stomach murmured in response. I climbed off and stroked his fuzzy neck. He didn't snap at me or bray. A new group of tourists wrapped scarves around their faces and squealed as their camels lurched from the ground. Number Seven would make the slow journey across the desert again, just plodding on. This time, as the leader.

Suzy Pope has travelled since the age of five and called herself a writer since the age of eight. It only just occurred to her to put the two things together a few years ago. Since then she has won various travel writing competitions and been published in *Wanderlust* magazine, *National Geographic Traveller* and Bradt's *Roam Alone* anthology. She continues to write fiction, but in a really slow, self-indulgent way.

Our Long-Eared Holiday Companion

Alison Ely

It was a hot, dusty December morning in Accra when Kweku, my husband, drove back with a surprise package on the front seat of the car. We were on holiday in Ghana with Fiona, our eight-year-old daughter, visiting Kweku's family. Fiona and I peered through the window and there, on the seat eating some carrots, was a rabbit.

'A rabbit?' I said. 'Why is there a rabbit on the seat?'

'A man was selling it by the roadside and it looked so cute that I had to buy it,' Kweku replied.

'But we're on holiday. How can we look after a rabbit?'

'Oh, I don't mean we should keep it ourselves. I want to take it to my brother in Elmina. He keeps goats. I'm sure he would like to keep rabbits, too. They breed quickly, you know.'

The rabbit looked up at me. It was rather cute with silvery-grey fur and floppy ears.

'What is it, male or female?' I asked.

'The man said it was a fine, healthy female.'

I opened the door and picked her up, still with a carrot clamped in her teeth.

'Well, she has to have a name if we are going to look after her for even a little while,' I said, stroking her long silky ear, before handing her to Fiona who was visibly delighted as she cuddled the ball of fur.

'What is a rabbit called in Fante?'

'*Asoasoa*,' said Kweku, pronouncing it 'a-swar-swar', 'and it means "long ears".'

'And what is the name for a girl born on a Thursday?' asked Fiona, today being Thursday. She was already familiar with the Ghanaian system of naming each person according to the day on which they were born.

'Yaa,' said Kweku, although it sounded like 'Yar'.

'So she is now Yaa Asoasoa,' I said triumphantly, relishing the rhyming sound of the name. Kweku looked relieved. For a minute he thought his 'surprise' had backfired.

'Hang on a minute,' I suddenly remembered, 'if we are all going away for the weekend, who will look after her?'

'She will have to come with us,' said Kweku, thinking he was saying something practical.

'Kweku,' I said, 'you are crazy.'

Adjoa, Kweku's cousin, in whose house we were staying, produced a sturdy plastic basket to serve as the rabbit hutch. The sides had open fretwork so the rabbit could see out and it also had a lid so she couldn't escape.

'But she has to exercise,' said Kweku. 'She can't stay in that small basket all the time.'

We decided to make her a lead from some string, so that she could nibble the grass but not run away. Within minutes she had slipped out of the string looped around her neck and had hopped away towards a hibiscus bush.

'What about a sort of waistcoat?' I suggested. 'It could fit around her body and we could tie the string to that.'

'Take her to the seamstress,' said Kweku, thoroughly enjoying the notion of a travelling rabbit in a waistcoat. So off we set to the local seamstress whose kiosk was nearby. Much to my amazement the seamstress didn't seem at all fazed by the prospect of making a waistcoat for a rabbit. She took Yaa's measurements, showed us a small offcut of printed fabric and quoted her price.

'Come back at 5 p.m.,' she said, 'and it will be ready.'

At 5 p.m. prompt, we were back at the kiosk where a sweet little waistcoat, with buttons down the back, was presented to us. We thanked the seamstress, paid our money and hurried back home for the fitting. Kweku held the rabbit while I placed the waistcoat over Yaa's front paws and did up the buttons on the back. It fitted perfectly. So far, so good. We tied the string to the metal ring that the seamstress had sewn to the back. Then we placed Yaa on the ground and watched. She nibbled the grass a bit and then she started to wriggle. Within seconds she had slipped out of the waistcoat and was hopping towards her favourite hibiscus bush. What a disaster!

Kweku retrieved Yaa and we sat down despondently in the courtyard.

'How about we make a sort of harness?' I eventually said. 'We could tie some of your shoelaces to the string to make it longer and fit the harness over her body.'

'We could give it a go,' said Kweku who promptly went to get some trainers which he unlaced. The harness proved a success and Yaa hopped happily on the grass, held securely with the aid of some well-knotted shoelaces.

The next morning we drove to Ada, a town at the mouth of the Volta River, where the broad estuary meets the Atlantic Ocean and where we intended to spend the weekend. I had read about an eco-camp of woven reed huts with thatched roofs set by the beach. The road was straight and the landscape was flat. It was really quite boring, miles of open plain on either side of the road, punctuated by the odd herd of cattle and a very odd tree that looked like a baobab. Yaa sat quietly in her basket on the floor in the back beside Fiona's feet, nibbling lettuce.

I was delighted when we eventually reached the eco-camp. As promised it was a collection of thatched huts with walls of woven reed. Inside each hut was a bed with a mosquito net. The toilet and showers were in a block nearby. I thought it was so romantic, set as it was beside a beautiful sandy beach by the ocean. Here and there coconut palms dotted the compound. A lovely breeze was blowing off the sea. Buying some drinks from a local bar we all walked down to the beach, with Fiona carrying Yaa in her basket. Sitting on the sand with our bottles of beer and cola, I let Yaa out and she shuffled around on the sand.

Suddenly she knocked over Kweku's bottle of Guinness. The frothy black liquid spilt out on to the sand, and Kweku grabbed the bottle before he lost too much. But the rabbit was already licking up the beer where it had fallen into the upturned bottle top. Having finished the Guinness, she looked up for more.

As the sun began to go down, we made our way back to the huts. I let the mosquito net fall and tucked it in around the mattress. Kweku unpacked the torch and we made our way through the shadowy camp to the shower room. There was no electricity and no running water, just a big tank and a few buckets. But it was a beautiful, clear night and I was enjoying my romantic hideaway. We showered beneath the stars in water warmed by the sun.

Back inside the hut it was very warm, the breeze having died away at sunset. Inside the mosquito net it was even warmer.

'What happened to "the cooling breeze from the ocean" that the guidebook talked about?' asked Kweku as he lay spread-eagled on the bed, already sweating. I lay on the bed in silence. Suddenly we heard the unmistakable buzzing of a mosquito. Kweku grabbed the torch and flashed it around wildly.

'Hold this,' he said, giving me the torch. With both hands he began clapping at the air.

'Got you!' he said triumphantly, opening his palms to reveal a squashed mosquito. 'Whose idea was it to stay in this mosquito-infested sweat lodge?' he grumbled. Throughout the night the mosquitoes buzzed, the heat intensified, and Kweku clapped his hands repeatedly. As the sun rose we were all grumpy and exhausted from too little sleep. Only the rabbit seemed content.

We packed our things, drove into the town and found a pleasant guesthouse surrounded by a colourful flower garden. We booked a room and managed to secretly smuggle the rabbit in amongst our luggage.

'Do you think they would throw us out if they found the rabbit?' I asked Kweku.

'Probably not, but I think we should keep quiet about it all the same.'

We found a new home for Yaa inside the wardrobe, but left the door open so she could enjoy her freedom. Leaving the rabbit with half a watermelon to eat, we headed out for the day. We hired a small motorboat to explore the river and ate a lunch of fried octopus on the beach before returning to the guesthouse – hot, sandy and tired, but happy. We found the rabbit happily hopping around the bedroom floor, having politely left little piles of droppings in the corners of the room.

We spent a very pleasant night at the guesthouse, only woken by the occasional scampering of the rabbit across the bedroom floor. She seemed to have created a mini-racetrack for herself. Leaving the confines of the wardrobe she would go skittering madly across the slippery tiled floor to the bathroom; there she rested before hopping back towards our bed where she hid for a while between our suitcases. A few minutes later she would dash off again, her little nails clicking and scratching on the floor. At one point Kweku said she climbed up on to his suitcase and then on to the bed beside him, but I thought he was dreaming.

Leaving the rabbit with a carrot for breakfast, we went out on to the terrace to eat our own. We were just finishing our last cup of coffee when a young man wearing overalls and carrying a broom appeared beside our table. He came towards me with a serious expression and, leaning forward, said in a low voice, 'Excuse me, Madam. I've swept your room, but I couldn't make your bed. The rabbit was asleep on it.'

Alison Ely is an artist from the UK who moved to Ghana with her husband in 2010. There they built a house on the beach where they now live with several dogs, cats and... rabbits. She is currently writing a book about her experiences travelling and living in Ghana.

From *Christian the Lion: the Illustrated Legacy*

John Rendall

In 1969 two young Australians, John Rendall and Ace Bourke, bought a three-month-old lion cub at Harrods department store in Knightsbridge. They called him 'Christian' and raised him at the World's End on the King's Road in Chelsea where a professional photographer named Derek Cattani recorded his adventures.

When Christian outgrew his London home George Adamson, of Born Free fame, agreed to rehabilitate Christian back into the wild in Kenya. It would be the first time an English-bred lion was to have this opportunity.

The following story of Christian's unique journey back to Kenya is an extract from a soon-to-be-published new book by John, with Derek's previously unpublished photographs, entitled Christian the Lion: the Illustrated Legacy.

When George Adamson finally secured the official approval for Christian to fly to Kenya we all celebrated and excitedly accepted the reality of Christian's rehabilitation into the wild.

At last we were off, and at Heathrow we were driven straight on to the tarmac, directly to the loading bay of the East African jet. In response to a request from the airline we attempted to weigh Christian, but it was fairly haphazard – we 'guestimated' that he weighed about 175 pounds and no-one at Heathrow was prepared to question that figure.

There was also a request that the film company making the documentary about Christian's rehabilitation should insure Heathrow for a million pounds while Christian was being transported. For a little cub that had cost 250 guineas the previous year, the idea that he might cause a million pounds' worth of damage at an international airport was pretty impressive; but there were no hitches and Christian was loaded safely on to the plane in his specially designed crate.

On 23rd August 1970 Christian landed on African soil, his ancestral homeland.

Unloading Christian in Nairobi was a prolonged process, just as frustrating as waiting for your luggage on a carousel after a long flight. Security and protocol for 'livestock' meant that Christian's crate had to be cleared by customs and immigration before he could be released into a secure holding area. It was immediately apparent that none of these officials was anxious to inspect Christian too closely, and from the attention Christian attracted it was also obvious that many of them had never seen a lion before, or if they had, certainly not one who was as tame as Christian.

George Adamson was there to meet us, anxious to meet Christian and to oversee Christian's unloading and transfer from the plane. At last we were to meet the great man, the guru of lions, the man who had rehabilitated Elsa, and the man who was going to rehabilitate Christian.

He was a much slighter figure than I had expected, almost dapper in his neatly trimmed goatee beard and pressed safari suit, but I later appreciated that this was for the film company and the special occasion of Christian's arrival.

He studied Christian carefully with his clear blue eyes.

He was impressed by his size and condition and, flatteringly, by his affection for Ace and me. He commented on Christian's thick coat and newly growing mane, explaining that no one-year-old Kenyan-born lion would be as large, thickly coated or prematurely maned.

The challenge of rehabilitating a fifth-generation lion from England, as he was to later write, fascinated George.

'The idea had appealed to me greatly, not only because it would save Christian from a lifetime of captivity, but also because it would be, in all probability, the first time an English-born lion had been returned to the life for which he was created. I felt confident that his inherited knowledge and instincts would soon assert themselves, given the chance, and in spite of his breeding.'

In the same letter – written in Kora and dated 15th July 1971 – George tells of his first reaction upon meeting Ace and myself.

'I must admit that I did not feel the same confidence about his two owners, when I heard that they would accompany Christian and stay for a few weeks in my camp. I had been led to believe they were very "mod" with long hair and exotic clothing. My first sight at Nairobi airport of pink bellbottom trousers and flowing locks did nothing to dispel my misgivings. But Ace and John soon restored my faith in the modern generation. Immediately, I sensed the bond of deep affection and trust between them and Christian. I know from experience how hard it must have been for them to leave Christian to face the inevitable dangers and hardships of a lion in the wild.'

After two days in the holding compound at Nairobi airport, where Christian became a huge attraction, it was time to set off for Kora, 250 miles north.

George had decided that the journey should be broken into two stages, so his old friend Nevil Baxendale was commissioned to build a temporary camp halfway to Kora, with a small enclosure for Christian.

When George backed his Land Rover into the holding compound at the airport, Christian was happy to jump into the back. He always loved driving around in cars in London and was bored by the cement enclosure at the airport. He must have been surprised to find straw to lie on in the back of the Land Rover, rather than the leather of a Mercedes or Bentley in London, and bemused by the wire-mesh panel between the front seats and the rear of the car. But this was George's 'standard equipment' fitting, necessary for transporting lions far less friendly or habituated to humans than Christian.

Christian was unfazed, though, and happy to stand and look out the back, again attracting considerable attention whenever we slowed in local traffic or refuelled with petrol.

The drive to Nevil's halfway camp was long and hot, and Christian lay panting in the back of the car while Ace and I took turns travelling with George, both of us eager to further gauge his reaction to Christian.

On the last part of the first day's journey, by now through parched and increasingly inhospitable countryside, I realised that Christian needed a loo break. I rather tentatively asked George – or Mr Adamson, as I was still referring to him at this stage – to stop so that Christian could 'stretch his legs', but George was sceptical. 'If he runs off here we'll never catch him.'

'He's not going anywhere,' I assured George and opened the rear of the Land Rover. Christian looked around gingerly, as it was hot and dry, and when he jumped down the road too was hot, dry and rocky – a far cry from the soft green grass of the Moravian Close in Chelsea. Christian sniffed the dry, unfamiliar air and went to the toilet, but he showed absolutely no interest in exploring the bush. When I encouraged him, he immediately jumped back into the Land Rover, and I closed the door behind him, and got back into the passenger seat. George had watched all this, quietly sucking on his pipe, and as we drove off he turned to me and said, 'That was quite remarkable. He is a fine young lion. Please call me George.'

Bravo Christian. I beamed with pride and couldn't wait to tell Ace.

When we arrived at Nevil's temporary camp we took Christian for his first proper walk in Africa, but this casual stroll soon took on a more significant element. Christian spotted something in the bush and immediately crouched and froze. It was a lost *gombi*, a domestic African cow. We watched in fascination as he stalked the gombi, creeping slowly forward, using the low bushes to conceal himself. Even though this was a domestic cow it had substantial horns that could be dangerous to an inexperienced young lion cub. Therefore George ran to get his Land Rover and drive it between the gombi and Christian. But Christian was not to be deterred; he dodged the car so, in desperation, George asked us to grab him. For the first time ever Christian snarled at us, giving us a very clear warning that he was not happy to have his first attempt at stalking frustrated.

Although we were rather shaken by this distinct warning, George was impressed by Christian's instinctive stalking and decided that it should be no more difficult to rehabilitate him than it had been to rehabilitate African-born lions.

That night in camp Christian was wonderfully affectionate; perhaps it was the excitement of this first stalking or to compensate for his earlier aggression. However, he was not impressed by sleeping on the ground, and he slept with a pillow and a paw on my face for reassurance. As Elsa had in George and Joy's various camps, Christian eventually took over a camp bed for himself. London was not too distant a memory even amidst all this excitement.

As we approached Kora the next day, George suggested we walk the last few miles on the track cleared by his brother Terence, so that Christian could start learning the smells and noises of his new home.

Terence had built a temporary camp at the Tana River while Kampi Ya Simba, The Camp of Lions, was being completed a few miles inland. We spent the first few days there walking and exploring with Christian. The Tana River dominates the Kora area and it is the Piccadilly Circus gathering place for all the wildlife in the area, particularly in the early evening.

Walking with Christian was exhilarating. With his collar and lead having been abandoned, he could now run free to investigate every new sound and smell. From the banks he could see hippos surfacing and blowing in irritation at the intrusion of strangers, and curiously watch the baboons and small vervet monkeys which barked and shrieked their warnings to the other animals.

George encouraged these walks, to toughen up Christian's pads, and help him acclimatise to the heat, because in only a few days Christian would be meeting the first lions he had seen since he had been separated from his sister at Harrods over a year ago.

We enjoyed our last few precious days alone with Christian.

Christian was successfully rehabilitated by George and disappeared into the wild in 1973. George and his assistant Tony Fitzjohn rehabilitated a further twenty-three lions at Kora National Park. Later on, after George was murdered by Somali bandits in 1989, the George Adamson Wildlife Preservation Trust was founded and, with Tony as field director, proceeded to fund and administer Mkomazi National Park in Tanzania. The focus of the Trust is on education and conservation, with emphasis on the breeding of black rhino and wild dog. As Tony quotes in his book, Born Wild, *'We all have a lot to thank Christian for.'*

ASIA

From *Travels on my Elephant*

Mark Shand

Tara was an elephant, and in Hindi her name means 'star'. With the help of a Maratha nobleman, Mark Shand purchased Tara and rode her over six hundred miles across India, from Konarak, on the Bay of Bengal, to the Sonepur Mela – the world's oldest elephant market. From Bhim, a mahout, Shand learned the skills of elephant driving. From his friend Aditya Patankar he learnt Indian ways. And with Tara, his new companion, he fell in love. So much so that decades after their travelling days were over, Mark Shand was still fund-raising and campaigning on behalf of Indian elephants. Travels on My Elephant *is the story of their epic journey across the dusty back roads of India.*

It was a glorious day as I watched her plodding in front of me, her tail swishing and her trunk shooting out from side to side, plucking at branches from overhead trees, flapping her great ears and munching with contentment. I felt wonderfully happy and patted her on her big, fat bottom.

'She really is lovely, isn't she, Aditya?'

'Yes, Mark.'

'No, I mean she is the most beautiful elephant in the world, isn't she?'

'Yes, Mark.' I could see I was going to drive him mad.

Considering it was our first day on the road, and that Tara was lame, we stopped and made camp by a wide river on the outskirts of a village called Nimpalla after covering a distance of only twelve miles. There are two basic requisites for a campsite when travelling with an elephant: one is water, for bathing and drinking, and the other is a stout, thickly leaved tree to which one can safely chain the elephant, to provide shelter from the sun and perhaps obtain fodder. We were lucky to find both. Beside the river, a row of ancient peepul trees stood like sturdy oaks. In a few minutes Gokul, with the agility of a monkey, and armed with an axe, had disappeared into the upper foliage and soon Tara's dinner came crashing to the ground.

For my benefit camps were, if possible, to be set up away from villages in the future. I had not yet become adjusted to the huge crowds that I knew our entourage would attract. I realised I had no right to complain. I was travelling in their country, probably camping on their land. An elephant with a foreigner was understandably fair game, but I was still too much of a tourist to tolerate such human curiosity. As countless pairs of eyes scrutinised my every move while I struggled with Aditya to put up our ridiculously complicated tent, I was not in the most charitable frame of mind.

'Go away,' I roared, waving my hands like a demented marionette. A hundred pairs of eyes blinked once, my tormentors settled themselves more comfortably on their haunches and waited patiently for the show to go on.

'They won't go,' Aditya remarked quietly. 'Just ignore them.'

'Well can't you frighten them or something?'

'Perhaps,' he suggested, 'if you removed those white socks and covered up those ridiculous blue underpants they might think that you're a human being instead of a creature from outer space.'

'I'm going to take a bath with Tara,' I added grumpily, noticing Bhim leading her towards the river.

'That, my friend, will probably cause a riot.'

Watching an elephant taking a bath is a delight in itself, but bathing with, or washing an elephant is something close to experiencing paradise. When I reached the river she was lying at full length with a contented expression on her face. Bhim and Gokul were busily scraping her with stones and the normally grey skin on her protruding backside was already turning black and shiny. Occasionally the tip of her trunk emerged like the periscope on a submarine, spraying them playfully with water before disappearing again and blowing a series of reverberating bubbles. I grabbed a suitable stone, and, forgetting my self-consciousness, joined in the fun.

After half an hour my arms were aching, my fingers were bleeding, but I felt absurdly proud. Bhim, sensing my eagerness, gave me the honour of cleaning her trunk, her ears and around her eyes, something which usually only the mahout, who is most familiar with the elephant, will undertake, due to the extreme sensitivity of these areas. However, he made sure that the *ankush*, or goad, was hooked around the top of one of her ears at all times.

'If Mummy feels that,' he explained, 'She give raja-sahib no trouble.'

She didn't, except at one moment when she took a liking to my underpants (I'm glad somebody did) and dragged them half down. This caused hilarity among the crowd, now squatting on the side of the riverbank. The whole process was then repeated on the elephant's other side. By means of a sharp command from Bhim, she lumbered to her knees and rolled over, creating a small tidal wave. Taking my new job as a mahout's assistant too zealously, I found out the hard way that Tara did not like to be scrubbed on the soles of her feet. She was extremely ticklish, and being winded by an elephant is not an experience I would care to repeat. I still had a lot to learn, I realised, or rather she had a lot to teach me.

At a small roadside house an old man with a long grey beard shuffled out from inside and stopped us. He sank to his knees, prostrating himself in front of Tara while she gently rubbed her trunk through his hair. A beautiful girl in a blood-red sari with a frangipani blossom behind her ear followed suit. After washing Tara's feet with water, she presented all of us with garlands of jacaranda flowers. There was a sudden sharp cry of pain behind us. A little boy, the girl's son, ran screaming to his mother, holding a small brown hand to his face. Blood seeped through his fingers. He had been standing too close to Tara's tail, watching it in fascination as she whipped it back and forth to brush off the flies. The thick, long, hard hairs at the tip had struck him on the cheek, splitting it like a melon. Aditya quickly pulled out the first-aid kit and after cleaning the deep wound, patched it with Elastoplast.

'I am sorry,' I said to the girl and the old man. 'I'm afraid it will leave a nasty scar.'

'Sorry, why be sorry?' he said quietly. 'Your elephant has done my grandchild a great honour. He has been blessed by Ganesh. He will always be lucky.'

Mark Shand's travel books include *River Dog, Queen of the Elephants, Skullduggery* and *Travels on my Elephant* for which he received the Travel Writer of the Year award. The journey directly led  to his foundation of Elephant Family – a charity established to protect the environment of the Asian elephant, tiger and orangutan. He died in 2014.

Finding Gobi

Dion Leonard

A s I walk towards the back of the plane, I take my seat next to a woman who can see from the worried look in my eyes that I am nervous.

'First time going to China?' she asks.

In fact, this is my second visit to China in as many months. I don't tell my fellow passenger, but I'm not worried about the long flight. I'm worried about a little stray dog I met over six weeks before whom I promised to bring home to live with me in Edinburgh, Scotland. I am flying back to find her in the city of Ürümqi in northwest China and I have no idea how I am going to do it.

I first saw Gobi as I completed the first of six stages of a 250-kilometre running race across the Chinese Gobi Desert. I had finished the stage in third position out of 101 starters and, whilst the first stage was only seventeen miles long, the weather had been cold, windy and slightly drizzly, which made life tricky as we crossed a terrain composed of rocky canyons, grassy fields and a huge climb over a sand dune known as 'The Dune of Barkhol'. The stage finished next to the base of the incredible Tian Shan mountain range; it was bitterly cold, yet thankfully I and six other competitors were to share a warm yurt for the evening instead of a traditional tent. I escaped the cold by heading to the yurt, deciding to have an afternoon rest inside my sleeping bag before dinner.

I was heading towards the campfire to prepare my evening meal when I noticed a small, sandy-coloured dog with a funny moustache walking around the fire. I remember thinking to myself as I watched another runner give the dog some food, *There's no way I'm going to feed it*. One of the rules of the race was that everyone had to carry all of their food, kit and equipment for the week to survive. I certainly wasn't going to give away any of my food, especially to a dog.

The next morning I was on the start line for stage two, which was a twenty-five-mile run over the Tian Shan mountain range and down into the Gobi Desert. I put my bag with all my food and kit on my back. With only a couple of minutes until the start of the race I went through my last-minute checks. Sunglasses clean, bag chest-straps done up, pockets zipped. I looked down to make sure my shoes and sand covers were connected – only to see the same little dog from the previous evening's campfire playfully biting on them. I shooed the dog away, but it thought I was playing a game and continued chewing. I asked if anybody knew whose dog it was, but by then the race had begun. I started running and looked down to see the dog running along with me, still nipping at my shoes.

Running over a cold, wet, windy and snow-capped mountain down into the heat and dryness of the desert took its toll on me. Nearly five hours later I could see the end of the stage in the distance and I was happy to be finishing for the day. To my surprise, there were some crew and runners clapping and cheering me over the finish line, which put a smile on my face. They continued clapping and cheering and I turned around, expecting to see another runner close behind me – but it was the little sandy-coloured dog, who'd managed to run the whole stage right behind me.

I was in complete amazement and disbelief that this tiny dog had run what was difficult for any human being to complete.

As I started to walk to my tent, the dog followed me and, once inside, collapsed next to me. I started to eat some dried meat and realised it must have been starving – I thus found myself feeding the dog that I'd said I wouldn't feed. She gulped down what I gave her and then positioned herself next to me and started to sleep. I still remember how bad she smelt, although I can't have smelt much better considering we don't shower during these week-long races. I could see that the dog was a girl and had a rash on her stomach; her coat was wiry and matted, and it was obvious she had lived a tough life already. I woke up a couple of hours later with the dog lightly snoring next to me. My tent mates had finished and were surprised to see the dog next to me. They told me it had followed some runners during the first stage of the race, and that's how it had ended up in the campsite.

Stage three began just like the previous day with the dog chewing on the sand covers of my shoes as we ran off from the start line together. I wondered if it would run with me all day again or whether the hundred-degree-Fahrenheit heat of the desert would mean she would stop along the way and that would be the end of our unique journey together. As I passed through the first checkpoint, it was clear the dog was on a new journey of her own that somehow involved me, and she wasn't looking back on her past existence.

I have a running superstition, which is to never look behind me during a race, but as I entered the waist-deep water of a wide river crossing with a strong current I heard squealing, barking and whining to the rear. I turned to see the dog running up and down the riverbank in complete anguish that I had left her behind. In a split second I decided to go back, pick her up and carry her to the other side. Little did I know this would be the start of a bond that would prove unbreakable. Later that evening, I named the dog 'Gobi' after the desert we were running through, and made her a promise to look after her, give her a better life and bring her home to Edinburgh.

After the race finished, I had to leave Gobi with someone in Ürümqi who offered to look after her while I made plans to take her to the UK. But now she has gone missing in a city of three million people. As the plane comes in to land, I look out to the vast city skyline.

I have been to the city before, as it's the closest airport to get to the Gobi Desert for the race, but I never wanted to return as it is a dirty, busy, overwhelming place that feels unsafe. But I have no choice. I am here for one reason: to find Gobi. When I received a phone call to say she had gone missing I was devastated. We'd been through so much together. Gobi had run 125 kilometres of the 250-kilometre race and it seemed my promise to her was broken.

I set about putting together a search team with volunteers who will walk the city looking for her and putting up reward posters in shop windows and on the windows of cars. It starts with one woman searching and quickly grows to hundreds looking day and night. I do local television and newspaper interviews and the story starts to spread on Chinese social media that a man has flown all the way back to China to look for a little dog. Soon the whole nation is looking for this little dog that they've never seen for a man they don't know.

After an emotional and dramatic rollercoaster ride of ten days searching the city we receive a message from a father and son saying they think they've found Gobi in an area we've been searching earlier that day. They had noticed the posters put up when the dog appeared and followed them to their home. I walk into the house and before I can say a word, Gobi has spotted me and comes running over, squealing, barking and whining just like she did on the riverbank during the race.

It will take a mountain of paperwork, medical procedures, operations and a considerable amount of money, sacrifice and commitment to get Gobi to her new home in Edinburgh in five months' time, but it is worth it. We've found each other twice and it is meant to be. My promise to bring Gobi home will be kept.

Dion Leonard is an Australian/ British ultra runner who lives in Edinburgh, Scotland. Dion has competed in, and completed, some of the most extreme running races around the world in the most inhospitable locations. In 2016 he  was running in the Gobi Desert when a stray dog followed him and this would change both of their lives forever. For more see: www.findinggobi.com.

Kenny

Dom Tulett

We clung close to the shore, testing our strength and that of the boat, and mapped along the eastern edge of the water. Visibility was poor – we could smell the smoke of the morning stoves of the houses in the hills, but could not yet see the fires.

Pokhara, the traveller hangout in Nepal's heartland, had disappeared behind us. The main backpacker strip of the town – the Nepal Mandala bookstore where I had bought a dog-eared copy of *Lost Horizon*, the Busy Bee café where travellers gathered under the prayer flags to drink European shots – all lights and life just hours before had been smothered by the dull hood of misty dawn. Trees on the shore appeared as ghosted outlines. Chilled air droplets hugged our fleeces and nipped at the napes of our necks. My hands numbed on the wet oars. It would become the day that Edmund Hillary died.

We had been told that on a clear day you could see the full majesty of the Annapurna range from the picturesque Phewa Lake, but my girlfriend and I saw none of that. As we sat clouded in grey, barely able to see the countryside around us, we felt another low on a difficult trip.

The last time we had been on a boat was in India, near the start of our three-month break wandering around South Asia. The twilight glide down the Ganges at Varanasi had started pleasantly but descended into hustle. We fared little better with other modes of transport: *tuk-tuks* diverted us to unrequested gift shops; taxis had broken meters and vague pricing strategies; an overnight bus to the border, without heaters or suspension, rattled us through an icy night, along rocky roads, lowering our defences, inviting on sickness. These were all indicators that we might be better off at home, playing it safe, leaving travelling to people bolder and braver than us.

In Delhi, we had walked the bustling lanes, reluctant to try anything, scared of everyone. A man in the street, seeing our white faces, started a conversation.

'Where are you from?'

'England.'

'Ah, Kevin Pietersen.'

I was encouraged by the cricket reference, but a second man tried to take advantage of the decoy, unsuccessfully snatching for my girlfriend's bag, before the two men ran off into the crowds. Back at the hotel we asked the desk clerk to help us book tickets for the train to Agra, first class. He looked concerned as we told him what happened in the street and warned us to be careful: 'There are bad people about.' We thanked him as he took our money and handed us our tickets, then set off for the station to find our seats located in a carriage marked with a large, white 2.

In a Kathmandu guesthouse we had discussed the possibility of giving in and heading home, doubting whether to give it one more day, keeping spirits up by listing the types of food we missed from home, still overcoming the nausea brought on by our most recent meal.

'Roast chicken.'

'Yes, and pizza.'

'Cheese sandwiches.'

'Spaghetti Bolognese.'

'But, actual spaghetti Bolognese – not minced, chewy chicken covered in weak tomato soup.'

'Yes!' I felt nauseous again. 'Red wine.'

But this was fools' motivation. We were instantly disappointed again at breakfast the next day: an improvised Western effort we prodded at before catching the bus to Pokhara and the make-or-break leg of our trip.

A flash of blue on a half-submerged tree cut through the gloom on Phewa Lake. It was bluer than the flanks of our rented row boat, shimmering and bright, like open ocean on a cloudless day. A kingfisher, our only company on the early waters, sat and surveyed the morning's prospects. It was the first bold colour we had seen. We rowed in for a closer look at the kingfisher and the little bird moved on to another branch further around the edge of the lake. A decision faced us: head for home or follow the bird. We followed, paddling on in cold pursuit.

We rowed slowly, edging closer to the kingfisher. All was silent except for the dip and slop of our oars entering and exiting the water, enough to alert the bird to our presence. He looked across at us, contemplating his visitors, then hopped along the southern edge of the lake, shifting from branch to branch, carefully and deliberately, eyeing the water closely, paying more attention to it than to us. We named him 'Kenny', alliteration overcoming imagination, and watched as he moved and paused, moved and paused, flitting from perch to perch, hoping for a better moment.

This sighting reawakened in me a decades-old memory: an eight-year-old boy with a Young Ornithologists' Club badge and a pair of heavy binoculars, standing in a blustery British countryside, straining for my first view of a kingfisher, distant and nervous, a blurry spot on a far-off riverbank. I remembered the rest of the world dissolving away, my attention focused on a single sight, my futile attempts to record the moment with my basic, twelve-reel, click-and-wind camera, and the kingfisher bolting for cover as our voices reached it on the wind.

As we followed Kenny, each leg of the trail warmed us slightly, the mist slowly beginning to burn through and the exertion of the paddling firing our muscles. Kenny showed us a new part of the lake, a section not visible from the town, an area we would not have gone near. Water buffalo cooled themselves by the shore as local fishermen collected their morning nets. Households came alive in the hills. Golden lights dotted the slopes. Children splashed in the shallows as the day warmed up. They called out to us and waved, and cheered and giggled when we waved back. Kenny was showing us new things, broadening our horizons, improving us as travellers. He raced out again across the water, his feathers glinting bright in a spoke of sunlight as he searched for a better view, arcing around our boat and deep into the mists covering the centre of the lake, inviting us to follow.

I remembered my childhood impression – one that still stands – that there's something special about a kingfisher: a daring, slender fizz of a bird, one that stands out in British airspace amongst the sparrows and blackbirds and pigeons. Even the colourful visitors to my grandparents' garden bird table – the robins, blue tits and goldfinches – didn't have the same exotic appeal. The occasional weekend trip to The Lodge nature reserve in Bedfordshire introduced the young me to the nuthatch and the jay and the pied wagtail, but a kingfisher was different – alluring, elusive, a prize. Kenny was all these things, and he was more. He was as close as we'd come to making a friend – an acquaintance, at least – on this trip. We had seen more of his world than we had of anyone else's, and stumbled upon one of the happiest experiences of our travels because of that.

The sun continued to bite through the haze and the mist gave up more of the lake's secrets. A tiny temple island, drifting burning incense, emerged out of the cloaked air. We found stone steps and a boat moored alongside, but no souls appeared to occupy the island, other than our friendly kingfisher. We saw him more closely now, his brilliant turquoise-blue wings and rich chestnut body, the strong red beak and sharp black eyes. He was proud, regal, impressive, focused. Kenny had become our guidebook, our map, our planner. Who better as a guide than someone who lived on the lake? He had no hidden agenda, no ulterior motive, no uncle who owned a carpet shop an unwanted detour away. Kenny appeared happy where he was, doing what he did. He didn't run and hide at the first hint of trouble, like his distant relative in my childhood encounter, and like we were considering.

One final time Kenny moved on. He skimmed the water's surface, dancing and playing as he flew for the northern shore, putting too much distance between us to be able to make it up. We watched in the direction he had flown. The skies had finally cleared, the mists dissolved, and the views revealed the Annapurnas from the lake, the pointed fishtail peak of Machhapuchhre standing above all else, white snow piercing blue, scraping the sky – magnificent. We paused and stared. Under a burning sun, the lake's waters stilled and offered another prize: a perfect reflection of the hills and mountains. It was a spectacular sight, one we would not have seen but for our avian companion, our little kingfisher guide, honest and true, who had not only opened up Phewa Lake, but showed us how to travel. He had not caught anything on our journey around the lake, but neither had he given up, continuing to hope and search, living for a better day. We wished him happy hunting, turned, cut the surface with our oars – dip and slop – and paddled home through the sparkling waters.

When we reached town, the news of Edmund Hillary's passing was filtering through. A sombre mood hovered over the town. We spent the rest of the day sitting quietly, reading on the shores. We made a plan to take a walking tour through the hills, booked a human guide, Guvinder, and met him early the following morning. He led us on a path up steep stone steps to watch the sunrise, along rhododendron-lined trails that ambled from village to village, to the huts with those smoking stoves where, eating a breakfast of warm tea and boiled eggs, picked from the fields and plucked from the coops, we looked down on the lake.

Dom Tulett lives with his family in Harpenden. On his daily commute to London he writes stories for his daughter about the places to which he's travelled. Alongside these, he is currently working on a novel set during the final months of the civil war in Sri Lanka. He is the 2017 winner of the New Travel Writer of the Year award from Bradt.

From *Unbeaten Tracks in Japan*

Isabella Bird

When Isabella Bird made her journey through Japan in 1878 at the age of forty-seven, she wrote: 'As no English lady has yet travelled alone through the interior, my project excites a very friendly interest among my friends, and I receive much warning and dissuasion, and a little encouragement... If I accepted much of the advice given to me, as to taking tinned meats and soups, claret and a Japanese maid, I should need a train of at least six packhorses.' She used several different horses over the course of the trip, travelling as she had previously done in Hawaii and the Rocky Mountains.

Yashimaya, Yumoto, Nikkozan Mountains 22nd June

Today I have made an experimental journey on horseback, have done fifteen miles in eight hours of continuous travelling, and have encountered for the first time the Japanese packhorse – an animal of which many unpleasing stories are told, and which has hitherto been as mythical to me as the *kirin*, or dragon. I have neither been kicked, bitten, nor pitched off, however, for mares are used exclusively in this district, gentle creatures about fourteen hands high, with weak hindquarters, and heads nearly concealed by shaggy manes and forelocks. They are led by a rope round the nose, and go barefoot, except on stony ground, when the *mago*, or man who leads them, ties straw sandals on their feet. The packsaddle is composed of two packs of straw eight inches thick, faced with red, and connected before and behind by strong oak arches gaily painted or lacquered. There is for a girth a rope loosely tied under the body, and the security of the load depends on a crupper, usually a piece of bamboo attached to the saddle by ropes strung with wooden counters, and another rope round the neck, into which you put your foot as you scramble over the high front upon the top of the erection. The load must be carefully balanced or it comes to grief, and the mago handles it all over first, and, if an accurate division of weight is impossible, adds a stone to one side or the other. Here, women who wear enormous rain hats and gird their kimonos over tight blue trousers, both load the horses and lead them.

I dropped upon my loaded horse from the top of a wall, the ridges, bars, tags and knotted rigging of the saddle being smoothed over by a folded futon, or wadded cotton quilt, and I was then fourteen inches above the animal's back, with my feet hanging over his neck. You must balance yourself carefully, or you bring the whole erection over; but balancing soon becomes a matter of habit. If the horse does not stumble, the packsaddle is tolerable on level ground, but most severe on the spine in going uphill, and so intolerable in going down that I was relieved when I found that I had slid over the horse's head into a mudhole; and you are quite helpless, as he does not understand a bridle, if you have one, and blindly follows his leader, who trudges on six feet in front of him.

The hard day's journey ended in an exquisite *yadoya*, beautiful within and without, and more fit for fairies than for travel-soiled mortals. The *fusuma* are light-planed wood with a sweet scent, the matting nearly white, the balconies polished pine. On entering, a smiling girl brought me some plum-flower tea with a delicate almond flavour, a sweetmeat made of beans and sugar, and a lacquer bowl of frozen snow. After making a difficult meal from a fowl of much experience, I spent the evening out of doors, as a Japanese watering place is an interesting novelty.

There is scarcely room between the lake and the mountains for the picturesque village with its trim neat houses, one above another, built of reddish cedar newly planed. The snow lies ten feet deep here in winter, and on 10th October the people wrap their beautiful dwellings up in coarse matting, not even leaving the roofs uncovered, and go to the low country till 10th May, leaving one man in charge, who is relieved once a week. Were the houses mine I should be tempted to wrap them up on every rainy day! I did quite the wrong thing in riding here. It is proper to be carried up in a *kago*, or covered basket...

When the horses arrived the men said they could not put on the bridle, but, after much talk, it was managed by two of them violently forcing open the jaws of the animal, while a third seized a propitious moment for slipping the bit into her mouth. At the next change a bridle was a thing unheard of, and when I suggested that the creature would open her mouth voluntarily if the bit were pressed close to her teeth, the standers-by mockingly said, 'No horse ever opens his mouth except to eat or to bite,' and were only convinced after I had put on the bridle myself.

Sarufuto

No! Nature has no discords. This morning, to the far horizon, diamond-flashing blue water shimmered in perfect peace, outlined by a line of surf which broke lazily on a beach scarcely less snowy than itself. The deep, perfect blue of the sky was only broken by a few radiant white clouds, whose shadows trailed slowly over the plain on whose broad bosom a thousand corollas, in the glory of their brief but passionate life, were drinking in the sunshine, wavy ranges slept in depths of indigo, and higher hills beyond were painted in faint blue on the dreamy sky. Even the few grey houses of Yubets were spiritualised into harmony by a faint blue veil which was not a mist, and the loud croak of the loquacious and impertinent crows had a cheeriness about it, a hearty mockery, which I liked.

Above all, I had a horse so good that he was always trying to run away, and galloped so lightly over the flowery grass that I rode the seventeen miles here with great enjoyment. Truly a good horse, good ground to gallop on, and sunshine, make up the sum of enjoyable travelling. The discord in the general harmony was produced by the sight of the Ainos, a harmless people without the instinct of progress, descending to that vast tomb of conquered and unknown races which has opened to receive so many before them. A mounted policeman started with us from Yubets, and rode the whole way here, keeping exactly to my pace, but never speaking a word. We forded one broad, deep river, and crossed another, partly by fording and partly in a scow, after which the track left the level, and, after passing through reedy grass as high as the horse's ears, went for some miles up and down hill, through woods composed entirely of the *Ailanthus glandulosus*, with leaves much riddled by the mountain silkworm, and a ferny undergrowth of the familiar *Pteris aquilina*. The deep shade and glancing lights of this open copse-wood were very pleasant; and as the horse tripped gaily up and down the little hills, and the sea murmur mingled with the rustle of the breeze, and a glint of white surf sometimes flashed through the greenery, and dragonflies and butterflies in suits of crimson and black velvet crossed the path continually like 'living flashes' of light, I was reminded somewhat, though faintly, of windward Hawaii. We emerged upon an Aino hut and a beautiful placid river, and two Ainos ferried the four people and horses across in a scow, the third wading to guide the boat. They wore no clothing, but only one was hairy. They were superb-looking men, gentle and extremely courteous, handing me in and out of the boat, and holding the stirrup while I mounted, with much natural grace. On leaving they extended their arms and waved their hands inwards twice, stroking their grand beards afterwards, which is their usual salutation.

Isabella Bird (1831–1904) was born in Yorkshire, England; her father was a clergyman and her mother was the daughter of a clergyman. She suffered from ill health and a doctor recommended a sea voyage. Her 1854 trip to America was a success and shortly afterwards she published a book about her experiences. It was the beginning of a lifetime of travelling and acclaimed writing, which established her as an explorer, and she was the first woman to become a Fellow of the Royal Geographical Society.

The Road to Blue Paradise

Lu Barnham

The ferry bulges and tilts with human life. Seth and I sit on the hot deck, elbow to elbow with fishermen, travellers, babies and baskets. The bustling harbour of Port Blair, capital of the Andaman Islands, disappears behind while flying fish scoot along the waves beside us in the neon-blue ocean and tiny Neil Island bobs tantalisingly on the horizon ahead. The passengers smile, shade their eyes from the sun, then brace themselves for the scrum to get off.

Neil Island has only three autorickshaws, rusty from years of sea breeze. We hail one and zip along the jetty, through a small marketplace, past the school, then out into the countryside, swerving to avoid the occasional thin hens dashing out across the dirt road. Cows tied up in the shade beneath palm trees watch us with luscious lashes and sleepy indifference. Old, thick cobwebs hang from the crooks of silver trees, where parakeets as bright as baubles chatter in the branches. At the end of the road stands a collection of rustic bungalows – Neil Island's 'resort'. How could we resist, having read their pamphlet, which promised our experience would be one of 'memorable pleasants', that snorkelling at the nearby beach would provide us with 'beautified visions of scenario' and that the on-site restaurant specialised in the presumably highly rare 'red snapper barracuda lobster crab'?

As soon as we arrive, we're adopted by two golden dogs, short-haired, rascally, energetic. They don't introduce themselves. They don't shyly approach and then warm up after pats and praise. They simply attach themselves to us, no questions barked. Seth favours the girl, and names her 'Megatron'. She is peachy soft, with fringes on her ears, and possessed of a gentle, wise air. My soft spot is for the young lad, a burly, muscular dog, with a Sinatra-esque confidence. I've named him 'Maverick', and both dogs are in our shadows constantly. If we smoke a cigarette on the balcony, they're underneath our chairs. If we head to the beach, they're at our sides. On the day we go out in a motorboat to snorkel and see dolphins, both dogs wait patiently on the shore. On the ill-fated morning when I punch a jellyfish by mistake, Maverick is there to offer commiserating licks. They watch with complete confusion as we make racetracks, obstacle courses and football pitches for hermit crabs.

The pleasures of canine company are only stretched thin one morning when a chance encounter makes me feel like David Attenborough. It's early and I'm walking alone on the sand. A washed-up sea urchin is dying so I return it delicately to the ocean with a twig. I paddle in the warm blue shallows, then perch on a large dead tree. Azure-and-white kingfishers shyly wait for me to leave so they can continue their hunting. I oblige, not thinking much, letting my feet take me around a corner, there to be confronted by a dinosaur. The enormous Andaman monitor lizard has its jaws and huge shoulders wrapped around a large turtle carcass. I stand and gawp at this charcoal-grey, hulking, prehistoric beast, his tail long, his tongue forked. He sees me and we freeze, staring at each other. When you live in a country where wildlife means hedgehogs, foxes and magpies, creatures such as this seem pure myth. I swear out loud. The monitor realises he's within waddling distance of deep undergrowth and makes a lumbering dash for it, his long tail cutting swathes through the sand and leaving small dunes, his legs flailing. Instinctively I follow, running, but he's soon out of sight, leaving me red-faced and surrounded by trees. I rush back to the bungalow, snatch my camera and return, hoping he'll be tempted back to the carcass.

Unfortunately, Megatron is thrilled to see me. Despite my best attempts, she will not be left behind. As I round the corner, hoping to capture an image of my glorious dragon, she trots merrily alongside me, spots the cautiously returning lizard and lets out a rapid concerto of barks, tearing across the beach ahead of me.

'Dog!' I cry, helplessly. The monitor takes one look at the orange nutcase and retreats, this time for good. I sit, defeated, by the mangled tree and Megatron curls up happily by my feet, snoring contentedly at a job well done.

As a young couple with no commitments, backpacking in Asia for six months, Seth and I like to think of ourselves as explorers, fantastically free, but this has been a laughable façade; the immediate bond between ourselves and these canines is every inch the intense, complicated love of the pet owner. One morning, we ride Neil Island's only bus into town for supplies. Handing over two rupees and taking our seats, we see two confused faces watching us through the dust. I feel a pang of guilt and then a flash of irritation; it's almost too much pressure these canines are exerting over us. Getting attached will make leaving harder.

At the marketplace, we find a blind grocer with a set of scales so ancient they'd look the part in the British Museum's Bronze Age exhibit. He sells us onions, limes, mangoes and tomatoes. There are tiny, bare-bone restaurants full of men playing cards. Lost cards trodden into the mud give the square a patchwork quality, always a diamond, a jack or an ace underfoot. We weave between dusty stalls piled high with trinkets, sifting our way through exercise books, tote bags and ointments. As I hand over coins for a tub of Tiger Balm to apply to our myriad mosquito bites, I watch the distant road, half expecting two little ginger dogs to appear. When they don't, I'm disappointed.

The owners of the empty thatched restaurant in the countryside are actually awake, so we stop for a chat. When do they open? Any time! What do they serve? Anything! When do they close? Whenever! Promising to return for dinner, we head back to the cabins and are met, huffily, on the path, by our two gingerbread friends, who escort us in raging silence back to the bungalow, where my shower is made slightly creepy by the resident green crab scuttling in and out of the drainage pipe.

Refreshed and hungry, we return to the restaurant with our dogs in tow. 'Blue Paradise' announces the brightly painted billboard. The combination of an island attitude and the presence of marijuana promises an evening joyous, soporific and strange.

The owner is Danesh, a friendly man who spends much of his day reclining in a deckchair looking supremely happy. Then there's Rajiv, the chef, an accomplished artist – his current masterpiece, a colourful painting of a crying child beside the ill-fitting quote, 'Don't worry, be happy!' becomes increasingly eerie the more one looks at it. There's also a teenage friend who talks little but grins constantly, and Ajay, a visiting cousin who makes a living from shark poaching. I don't feel like smoking so I drink a warm beer instead. The small talk is most preoccupying. Somebody points out that there are no potatoes on the island, which is met with universal hilarity. A gentle argument breaks out about whether or not the beautiful black birds known as racket-tailed drongos drag their tail feathers along the ground to trick ducks into following them around. When Ajay adds that drongos use their tail feathers to fish, I suspect we have left the factual world behind and entered some kind of gloriously goofy dimension. It takes two hours for dinner to reach the table (we suspect the chef has gone to the beach with a flashlight to capture the ingredients), but when it does arrive, Seth declares the coconut crab is the best meal he has eaten in his life – a fine turnaround, since we have been unable to track down any of the elusive red snapper barracuda lobster crabs. Beneath our feet, Maverick and Megatron recline, while the restaurant puppy, Magnet, also orange and no doubt a relative, tugs at their ears and crawls on their backs.

On our last day on the island, I find Seth fussing over Megatron on the porch. She has a torn ear. There must have been a bad fight last night. Protectively, Maverick sits alert and serious at the edge of the porch. I stroke him, but he doesn't seem to notice. We're just temporary owners, I realise, and island life can be hard for a dog. These two seem like honorary members of the resort team, but I doubt there's anybody who'd declare genuine ownership. They're hobos, stranded on a minuscule island in the remote Andaman Sea.

The same night, as the four of us walk back from another fun dinner with the Blue Paradise gang, Maverick leaves the path and runs off into the night. A few moments later there are sounds of fighting and yelping. Back at the bungalow, Megatron is curled happily under Seth's chair. Yawning, Seth climbs into bed, but I stand on the porch, worried. I'm aware of being absurd, frowning into the night like an anxious mother waiting for a teenage son to return from a night on the town. I'm still on the porch a whole hour later when Maverick returns, exhausted but unscathed, letting me stroke his golden coat as he snuggles down to sleep beside my toes. I stub out my fourth cigarette. This dog is turning me into a chain smoker.

As we leave Neil Island, fortifying our nerves for the crowded ferry onwards, I know the dogs will be fine. It's us who have grown needy, wanting to smuggle them in our backpacks. For the first time, they don't try to follow us. They'll have befriended new humans by the time we hit the opposite shore, I suspect. That's their nature – it's what we love about them – but it doesn't stop me cynically observing their indifference.

Two years later, on a rainy Oxford afternoon, Seth comes home to our flat, grinning, holding a friend's photograph. She, too, was lucky enough to discover Neil Island, and to find a little bungalow at the end of that dusty trail. And there in the background of her holiday snap are two orange dogs, a teensy bit more ragged and a small degree greyer. Our island hobos, still leaving paw prints on the road to Blue Paradise.

Lu Barnham is the author of two books. *An African Alphabet* chronicles her journey across Africa by public transport, while *The Cicada's Summer Song* describes her twelve-hundred-kilometre pilgrimage to Shikoku's eighty-eight temples in Japan. Born in Yorkshire, Lu now lives in New South Wales, Australia. To follow her travels visit: www.lubarnham.com.

Rani and Me

Harjeet Johal

If elephants could roll their eyes, shake their heads and tut, then the one I was standing opposite would have done it – and I wouldn't have blamed her. I was over-coiffured, over-fragranced and about to be on her back for the next few days.

Except for the occasional slow sway of her head, Rani stood motionless in the warm, October morning sun in India's northern jungle. Her arrival had been less serene: the foot-tall grass all around her had been completely flattened, as had anything that had called it home. The mahout then said something – a lyrical twist of Hindi that I couldn't understand – and she responded, lowering her trunk. He hopped on and she lifted him up. The wiry man scrambled up Rani's face, twisted and then flung himself behind her ears. With a cheeky smirk and a jab of his finger he gestured to my friend and me that we follow him up.

I was game and began taking off my blazer. The man's jesting smile turned to a blaze of fear – Rani looked worried, too. The Hindi became more frantic, the mahout's arms flapping wildly in a cross; then he pointed to a small mound alongside Rani. I got the idea that, upon reflection, they would prefer us to board that way, the beginners' way. So we did.

With legs stretched out in front and hats firmly fixed, we leaned back into our howdah, and with a gentle barefoot tickle behind the ear,

Rani moved. Followed by two more elephants, one carrying our camp and one carrying our luggage, we rocked side to side in a soothing rhythm as she stamped a path deeper into the Jim Corbett National Park. This wasn't a road well-trodden: the grass soared up and giant baggy leaves arched down. We dipped forward, scooted across, leaned inwards and made way, continuing through a glorious tunnel of green for hours and hours.

Bugs buzzed above, creatures rustled ahead. There was endless squeaking, squawking, crying and calling. Things dropping, branches snapping; paws running and claws clawing. It was deafening. I had been to India many times, but this was an India I had never seen or heard before – it was almost totally empty of people, yet uncontrollably alive. The mahout occasionally whispered a near-silent song that I couldn't understand, but my friend and I didn't swap a word. What possibly could we say that was more interesting than what we were hearing around us?

Rani's relentless pace never slowed. Occasionally she would thrust her trunk out to the side to grab some leaves. It was her mid-journey snack.

Finally, she began to slow and then stop. The mahout sprang off; we tumbled off. I patted Rani as a 'thank you'. She said nothing and just chewed on some nearby greenery. She still wasn't convinced that I was worth the bother.

The rush of water and the promise of food led me away, up a slight hill and then down a steep bank.

I am able to rough it, but I prefer not to. Fortunately, lunch demonstrated that I needn't have worried. For set on the pebbled bank of the tumbling Kosi River was a grand table with flowing white tablecloth, lace parasol and cushioned chairs.

The noise of the busy river swallowed the need for words. We both just sat, munched, stared and listened. I wanted to take in all I could from this new country, this parallel, secret India that I felt I had found by accident. This place wasn't the land of my ancestors; it wasn't bound up with traditions and superstitions. It had nothing to do with any of us.

Rani and her friends were chomping on something solid when we arrived back. Her mouth was wedged slightly open, giving her an unintentionally gummy smile. She reminded me of my grandma without her dentures.

'We had three courses and a brocade tablecloth, Rani,' I joked. She didn't find me funny.

The camp was set up before we arrived, high on a hill. My tent was fit for a dowager countess – complete with a mahogany bed, wardrobe and writing desk. I felt quite at home.

The cliché about stars on a clear night is one worth repeating again and again and again, as it's never completely possible to do the scene justice. I held my wine, looked up at the black sky that was congested with diamonds, and looked back down again. Once was enough – I'd never forget that sight.

The next day began well with Rani stomping our route through the brittle undergrowth. The mahout was whispering his usual tune, but only after a wave of Rani's trunk and him replying with a giggle and a pat did I realise that it wasn't a song at all; it was conversation. The mahout and his old friend Rani were constantly chatting in a language only they understood. I felt a pang of jealousy.

Out of everything we had seen that morning, it was a giant flying bug which captivated me the most. Black, bristly, as noisy as a freight train and full of legs, it was easily the size of a tennis ball. It flew slowly and not very elegantly. It was like a fat, drunk man stumbling around our heads. I had never seen anything like it. This new land had strange and wonderful lifeforms. 'What is it called?' I asked our guide. I was hoping for some elaborately named, extremely rare creature I could tell all my friends about.

He glanced slowly and expressionlessly at the little alien. 'Big bug,' he replied, before looking away. Oh well.

With the big bug behind us, we were about to leave a clearing when the mahout pulled Rani to a sudden stop. He held out his arm to make us still. He had heard a rustle. Rustles fill seasoned explorers with fear and delight in equal measure. Hearts pounded under shirts, backs sweated under blazers; Rani became an immovable grey solid. What could it be? I was hoping for an Asiatic lion. Or a bear of some kind.

We had neither fear nor delight when we saw what it was. The arm was lowered and Rani snorted in disgust: it was human. Two humans.

'Hello!' the man human called out. The woman human was waving wildly behind. We didn't wave back. The sun bounced off their blonde hair and disturbingly white teeth. They were, predictably, appropriately dressed in eleven shades of khaki. Strung around their necks were every type of photographic device.

'We've broken down!' the lady said. It was then that I realised that they were English, from Newcastle. An annoyed guide then emerged from the bush. He rattled off something to our guide, whom he greeted with a wave. Apparently, their jeep had broken down and they needed a lift to the nearest track. Given that we had three elephants, it was hard to refuse.

Rani was not impressed as the Geordie hitchhikers jumped on. Their cameras clanged together as they sat. Rani started moving and they started talking. They didn't stop. They passed commentary on every single thing they saw. Didn't they know that this wasn't a country for words?

A few moments later, another rustle. The tension was palpable. Even the hitchhikers shut up. We were all just hoping: no more humans. And then, on cue, out walked a tiger.

The hitchhikers were already focusing the zoom of one of their long lenses. I looked over to my friend. We had packed seven blazers between us, but no camera. An annoyed guide at the base camp had managed to find a disposable camera for us. My friend shook his head and folded his arms. So I lifted up the little green cardboard box, and began winding the small plastic wheel. As the pistons fired on their nuclear-powered shutters, I waited for my moment. Then, with the tiger perfectly framed, I pressed. The pathetic, plasticky click echoed around the world. It was the sound of utter humiliation. It was a new low for Rani.

We got rid of the humans and their metric tonne of technology a little later. As the sky began to look exhausted we stopped at the side of a small stream.

'We are not supposed to be here, but it should be OK,' the guide said, intriguingly, as he led us through low grass and up a steep hill. It was heavy going, but his nervousness made me excited as to what was ahead. After ten minutes of twists and a bit of scrambling, we made it to a plateau in the rock. Out of one of the caves shot a cat – a domestic ginger cat wearing a rag collar. Following him was a man. He was naked except for a cloth around his waist. His hair was knotted and his beard was wild. He was happy to see us. We followed the man and the guide to an overhang of rock which served as his day lounge. He gestured for us to sit, and we did. 'Tea, tea!' he said, enthusiastically, gesturing to a saucepan on a dead fire.

Over tiny beakers of ginger tea, he spoke in near-perfect English about the jungle and his cat, named 'Tiger'. My granddad had told me about hermits like him who remove themselves from the world and seek refuge in the wild. Some call them *sants*, or saints. They believe that decades of prayer and isolation put them in direct contact with God. I wasn't sure about any of that, but he had a story. Something had driven him to run away from life. He didn't have the eyes of a happy man. I felt sad as we rejoined a chomping Rani. On that day people had invaded her world more than they should.

The final day was an early start. My friend claimed he was ill. He wasn't ill at all. He just wanted to drink wine, read his book and dream that he was a colonial governor during the Raj. He, along with my luggage elephants, stayed at the camp which we would return to at the end of the day.

So it was just Rani and me. Gone were the blazer and brogues. Standing opposite her in the dawn mist, I could tell she approved. The mahout gestured to her trunk. Without giving them a moment for retraction or regret, I stepped on. Up I went! Rani and I were finally friends.

Once behind her ears, I refused to move. I drove for hours. I wasn't really bothered about what I was seeing; I just loved being where I was. I fed my new friend sugar beet and calmed her when she heard the yell of a wild bull elephant. It was nice to see her showing some emotion. And, as the sharp sun began to give way to the haze, and as my friend finished his second bottle of wine, I stripped down to my boxer shorts and joined Rani in the river for her bath. My transformation was complete.

The drive back to Delhi was a sad one. I had made a friend whom I was never going to see again and glimpsed an India I was never going to experience again. As we approached the airport the traffic started to slow. I looked to see what was causing the problem. Ahead, a holy man wrapped in saffron robes was walking, holding a piece of string to which a painted cow was attached. That cow was joined by string to a smaller cow. And bringing up the rear of this procession, again attached by string, was the holy man's wife. This was the India I knew: a place locked in an unbreakable assignation with the unfathomable. I much preferred Rani's country.

Harjeet Johal is a writer from Nottingham, England. Travelling all over the world, many of his adventures have involved animal travel companions – from elephants in India through to donkeys in Bolivia and a camel called Camilla in the Sahara.

From *Across Coveted Lands*

Henry Savage Landor

Henry Savage Landor published Across Coveted Lands *in 1902, describing his overland journey from Flushing (Holland) to Calcutta. In this extract he is crossing the Great Salt Desert of Persia.*

A whole day was spent in preparing for the journey, and when 4th November came, shortly before midnight my provisions were packed upon my camels, with an extra load of fowls and one of fruit, while on the hump of the last camel of my caravan were perched, in a wooden box made comfortable with straw and cotton wool, two pretty Persian kittens, aged respectively three weeks and four weeks, which I had purchased in Kerman, and which, as we shall see, lived through a great many adventures and sufferings, and actually reached London safe and sound, proving themselves to be the most wonderful and agreeable little travelling companions imaginable. One was christened 'Kerman', the other 'Zeris'.

The Persian cat, as everybody knows, possesses a long, soft, silky coat, with a beautiful tail and ruff, similar to the cats known in Europe as Angora, which possess probably longer hair on the body. The Persian cats, too, have a longer pencil of hair on the ears than domestic cats, and have somewhat the appearance and the motions of wild cats, but if properly treated are gentleness itself, and possess the most marvellous intelligence. Unlike cats of most other nationalities, they seem to enjoy moving from place to place, and adapt themselves to fresh localities with the greatest ease. If fed entirely on plenty of raw meat and water they are extremely gentle and affectionate and never wish to leave you; the reason that many Persian cats – who still possess some of the qualities of wild animals – grow savage and leave their homes, being principally because of the lack of raw meat which causes them to go a-hunting to procure it for themselves. The cat, it should be remembered, is a carnivorous animal, and is not particularly happy when fed on a vegetable diet, no more than we beef-eating people are when invited to a vegetarian dinner.

Isfahan is the city from which long-haired Persian cats, the *burak*, are brought down to the Gulf, and from there to India, but the Kerman cats are said by the Persians themselves to be the best. The white ones are the most appreciated by the Persians; then the blue (grey) ones with differently coloured eyes, and the tabby ones. Mine were, one perfectly white, the other tabby.

At midnight I said goodbye to Major Phillott, whose kind hospitality I had enjoyed for four days, and began my slow and dreary march on camelback. Swung to and fro till one feels that one's spine is breaking in two, we wound our way down from the Consulate at Zeris, skirted the town, now asleep and in a dead silence, and then turned northeast among the barren Kupayeh Mountains.

We had a fine moonlight, and had I been on a horse instead of a camel I should probably have enjoyed looking at the scenery, but what with the abnormal Persian dinner to which I had been treated in the afternoon – what with the unpleasant swing of the camel and the monotonous dingle of the camels' bells – I became so very sleepy that I could not keep my eyes open.

There is very little style to be observed about riding a camel, and one's only aim must be to be comfortable, which is easier said than done, for camels have so many ways of their own, and these ways are so varied, that it is really difficult to strike a happy medium.

On 6th November we were some fifty miles from Kerman. Again when midnight came and I was slumbering hard with the two kittens, who had made themselves cosy on my blankets, the hoarse grunts of the camels being brought up to take the loads woke me up with a start, and the weird figure of the camel man stooped over me to say it was time to depart.

'Hrrrr, hrrrr!' spoke the camel man to each camel, by which the animals understood they must kneel down. The loads were quickly fastened on the saddles, the kittens lazily stretched themselves and yawned as they were removed from their warm nooks, and Sadek in a moment packed up all my bedding on my saddle.

Four camels of the combined caravans had been taken ill with fever and had to be left behind. Their cries from pain were pitiful. Owing to the abundant dinner we got here, with lavish supplies of meat, fruit – most delicious figs, pomegranates and watermelons – of which we partook more copiously than wisely, all the men got attacks of indigestion, and so did my poor little kittens, who had stuffed themselves to their hearts' content with milk and the insides of chickens; so that when night came, everybody being ill, we were unable to make a start.

At sunset, with the sudden change in the temperature, and the revulsion from intense dryness to the sudden moisture of the dew, a peculiar feeling took possession of me, and I could feel that I was fast inhaling the miasma of fever. The natives shut themselves up inside their houses – for sunset, they say, and sunrise are the times when fever is contracted – but we were out in the open and had no protection against it. It seems to seize one violently from the very beginning and sends up one's temperature extremely high, which produces a fearful exhaustion, with pains in the ribs, arms and spinal column.

The altitude of Lawah is 4,420 feet and therefore the nights are terribly cold in contrast to the stifling heat of the day. I had wrapped myself up in my blankets, shivering with the fever that had seized me quite violently, and the kittens were playing about near my bed. My men were all sound asleep and only the occasional hoarse roar of the squatted camels all round our camp broke the silence of the night. I eventually fell asleep with my hat over my face screening it from the heavy fall of dew.

Suddenly I woke up, startled by the kittens dashing under my blankets and sticking their claws into me and making a fearful racket, and also by some other animals sniffing my face. I jumped up, rifle in hand, for indeed there were some wolves visiting our camp. One – a most impudent rascal – was standing on one of my boxes, and another had evidently made a dash for the white cat; hence the commotion.

The wolves bolted when I got up – I could not fire owing to the camels and people being all round – but the kittens did not stir from their hiding place until the next morning, when in broad daylight they cautiously peeped out to see that the danger had passed.

With the coming day the gruesome reality had to be faced, that one and all of my party had contracted fever of the desert in more or less violent form, even the kittens, who sneezed and trembled the whole day. Some of the camels, too, were unwell and lay with their long necks resting upon the ground and refused to eat. The prospects of crossing the most difficult part of the desert with such a sorry party were not very bright, but we made everything ready, and at ten o'clock in the evening we were to make a start.

I purchased here a third and most beautiful cat – a weird animal, and so wild that when let out of the bag in which it had been brought to me, he covered us all over with scratches. He was three months old, and had quite a will of his own. When introduced to Master Kerman and Miss Zeris, there were reciprocal growls and arched backs, and when asked to share their travelling home for the night there was evident objection and some exchange of spitting. But as there were four corners in the wooden box and only three cats, they eventually settled down, one in each, watching the newcomer with wide expanded eyes and fully outstretched claws, merely for defensive emergencies, but otherwise quite peacefully inclined.

I had arranged with the caravan that accompanied mine to carry fodder for my camels, as there was no grazing for the animals here. Large cloths were spread on which straw and cottonseeds were mixed together, and then the camels were made to kneel round and have a meal.

[Twenty miles later] I was much struck by the really marvellous intelligence of cats. We hear a lot about dogs finding their way home from long distances by using their sense of scent (how far this explanation is correct we have no time to discuss), but of cats the general belief is that if they are taken away from home they seldom find their way back. This may be the case with cats that have always been shut up in some particular house, but it is not that they do not possess the intellect to do so in their natural state. Here is an instance.

On letting the cats loose when we halted, the newly purchased one attempted to make his escape. I was watching him carefully.

He did not do this in a haphazard manner, running here and there as a dog would, but jumped out of the box, took his bearings with great calm and precision and in a most scientific manner, first by looking at the sun, and then at his own shadow, evidently to discover whether when shut up in the box he had travelled east or west, north or south, or to some intermediate point. He repeated this operation several times with a wonderful expression of intelligence and reflection on his little face, and then dashed away with astounding accuracy in the direction of Lawah town. Mind you, he did not at all follow the track that we had come by, which was somewhat circuitous, but went in a beeline for his native place and not a second to the left or right of the direct bearings which I took with my prismatic compass to check his direction. Sadek and the camel men went in pursuit of him and he was brought back.

This seemed so marvellous that I thought it might be a chance. We were then only twenty-two miles from Lawah. I repeated the experiment for three or four days from subsequent camps, until the cat reconciled himself to his new position and declined to run away. I took the trouble to revolve him round himself several times to mislead him in his bearings, but each time he found his correct position by the sun and his own shadow, and never made a mistake in the absolutely correct bearings of his route.

A remarkable fact in connection with this is that the most ignorant natives of Persia, men who have never seen or heard of a compass, can tell you the exact direction of places by a very similar method, so that there is more in the process than we think.

It is rather humiliating when we reflect that what we highly civilised people can only do with difficulty with the assistance of elaborate theodolites, sextants, artificial horizons, compasses and lengthy computations, an ignorant camel man, or a kitten, can do practically and simply and always correctly in a few seconds by drawing conclusions on facts of nature which speak for themselves better than all the scientific instruments we can manufacture.

Arnold Henry Savage Landor (1865–1924) spent his childhood in Florence, Italy, and left for Paris at age fifteen to study. He then travelled the world, including America, Japan and Korea, painting landscapes and portraits, and on returning to  England was invited to Balmoral by Queen Victoria to recount his adventures and show his drawings.

AUSTRALASIA

Piloted across
the Indian Ocean

Sarah Outen

M y first solo ocean-rowing experience came in 2009, when I spent four months rowing across the Indian Ocean from Australia to Mauritius. My routines revolved around rowing, eating and sleeping and looking after the boat and myself. There was a beautiful and arduous simplicity to it, all within the realms of a boat small enough to park on a two-car drive, set to the rhythm of the ever-changing weather and waves. It was a dynamic world of textures and sound, horizons variously roughed, shrinking away into the distance on mirror-flat days or looming close in walls of water and surf. It was magic. Elemental. Raw.

Within a few weeks I felt like I had settled into my new world. I was more of the ocean than of land.

It was day ten when I first met the Tweedles. It was a mirror-calm sort of day, sun blazing down and the ocean a delicious amalgam of blues and turquoise – my favourite weather. Everything was crying out for me to jump in and swim, except the even louder, shoutier part of my head which worried about sea monsters nibbling my toes. Or even just the chance of seeing a sea monster. I so wanted to do it and my muscles ached for the coolness, yet my logical head was trawling up memories of being swept out to sea on a rubber ring as a child when I had been too scared of jellyfish to swim back to the beach and had to be pulled back to shore by a watching bystander.

'I'm going swiiiiiiming!' I squealed half nervously and half excitedly to my video camera as I tied on my extra-long safety line and donned my mask and snorkel. I stood on the edge of the boat, leaning back on my safety rails. One last look for fins and sea monsters. A bird wheeled in the distance, foraging for dinner, but there was nothing and no-one else; it was silent and empty. Instead of jumping in with a whoop I just froze, eventually stepping back on deck for a quick pep talk. I took a deep breath and stood up for another go, but again, I didn't get any nearer to the water. Kneeling down, I stuck my head under the surface, just to reassure myself that it was OK. Of course it was, so I got back up on my perch, ready to jump. Once more, I froze. And so there I remained, egging myself on until the boat had keeled over so much that I slipped and fell in with a very inelegant splash.

I was in the ocean just long enough to register that it was both very blue and way too deep to comprehend, when a little black-and-white-striped fish looked up at me. I squealed and leaped out, my first foray ending almost before it had started. I was so chuffed to have made it into the water and confident that I would jump in to fix something if I needed to. But I was more than a teensy bit scared. Scared of what exactly, I am still not too sure, for the fish was only eight centimetres from nose to tail. Peering back over the side, my head under the water, I was enchanted, and all the more so when another fish appeared. In their stripy little jackets they were calling out to be named Tweedledum and Tweedledee, so I did. Over the coming days, as we got further off the continental shelf and more of them appeared, I appointed their stripy collective the 'Tweedles'. At their peak, they numbered about thirty, led by the impressive Monsieur Tweedle Le Grand, the largest of them all at thirty centimetres.

A perfect size for dinner, one might think, but I had already declared that fish were friends and not food. In the early days I tried fishing with the handline my brothers had given me, but was secretly pleased that I didn't catch anything; the thought of eating one of my friends was awful. Besides, I had already lost my only suitable cooking pot overboard and, apart from the Tweedles, the other fish I had seen were far too big for me and I would hate to waste one. Given that the world's fish stocks are being plundered so brutally that they are set to collapse in the next thirty years, I felt I ought to do all I could to save them, not eat them.

Pilot fish by name and pilots by nature, these stripy fish are escorts of most ocean wanderers – boats, beasts and other flotsam – and they followed my boat for thousands of miles. Even through rough weather they managed to stay close by and I was always excited to pop outside after a storm to say hello to them again. Because obviously I talked to them. People laughed when I told them that the fish were my friends, but it was true – I talked to them and was very upset with myself when one of them got bopped on the nose by my oar, leaving it with a pink scar. Their bow riding always made me smile, too, mostly because I had never considered that we might travel fast enough to create a bow wave. While the conversation might have been a bit limited, it was always good to see them rushing over to nibble the remnants of dinner when I washed my cooking pot overboard or to have them school around me on the rare occasions I went for a swim. To be stretched out and floating was delicious and to look down into the unfathomable depth beneath me was, well, unfathomable – as if I were suspended in time, all notion of the real world frozen, and no link to it but for my lifeline of webbing clipping me on to the boat.

We bobbed along with the swell while I worked to scrape off the growth around the rudder and clean up the water-maker inlet; it would be a mini-disaster if that got fouled up. The Tweedles wiggled in close to check me out, chasing the evicted barnacles as they sunk into the murk. It was entertaining and comforting somehow to have my little troupe of striped fish close by. With no-one else around, I found that I held on to all signs of life very tightly, mesmerised by anything that flew or swam or floated past.

As I approached the continental shelf on the other side of the ocean, the sea and the sky began to change. Clouds towered above islands to my north. The waves changed shape and the sea became darker and greener. The Tweedles must have noticed the cues as well, one by one dropping away. For a few days I tried to coax the final solitary stripy follower with bits of food, until the morning of day 118 I found that he, too, had deserted. Whether he had succumbed to the food chain or joined another caravan of fish or boat on some other journey I didn't know.

But I was glad to have had their company.

Sarah Outen has spent months rowing solo across the world's oceans over the last decade, often as part of longer human-powered journeys. She has written two books, *A Dip in the Ocean*, of which this is an adapted excerpt, and *Dare to Do*. For more info: sarahouten.com.

Starboard

Michael Howorth

In the late 1960s almost every British ship sailing the oceans under the red ensign carried a cat. Aboard our general cargo ship – one of the three hundred-plus that made up the then mighty Peninsular and Oriental Steam Navigation Company, more commonly called P&O – we had a ginger moggie called 'Starboard'. He was called Starboard because he had one bright green eye on his right-hand side while the other was slightly yellow.

Starboard loved cheese or at least we always thought he did. Why? Because, every night, after dinner, just as the officers would get to their cheese course, Starboard would come to the wardroom and collect his hunk of cheddar. We never actually saw him eat it because he always disappeared off with it carefully carried in his mouth.

One evening after dinner, if only to relieve the boredom of a twenty-one-day passage across the Pacific, I and a fellow officer followed Starboard as he made his way purposely along the gently rolling deck towards the bow of the ship. It was a balmy night with calm seas and a clear black sky studded with trillions of stars overhead and, this far forward, we were removed from the sounds of the ship's engines. All we could hear was the frothing of the sea as the bow cleaved its path forward through the ocean. We crept silently along the deck, frightened that any noise we created might upset Starboard and put him off his daily routine. When Starboard came close to the bosun's locker, where the crew stowed the paint and ropes they used every day, his trot slowed to a leisurely walk and then he stopped.

We watched enthralled as Starboard dropped his cheese into the scupper – the drains on the side of the deck – and then he sat down, tucking his tail neatly around his front paws. He sat still as a statue intently staring at the cheese. We waited patiently too, a few feet back so as not to disturb the tableau. Ten minutes passed and then ten more and, just as I was thinking about returning to the comforts of my cabin, a small rat appeared from within the paint store and approached the cheese. Wallop went Starboard's paw and the rat was caught. Minutes later, main course finished, Starboard tucked into his cheese course just as the officers had half an hour earlier!

Needless to say, when we recounted our night-time sortie to our fellow officers in the wardroom they were enthralled and Starboard immediately acquired a new cult status. He was promoted from ship's moggie to 'Chief Rat-Catching Cat', which was of course the primary reason for the tradition of ships carrying cats as part of their sea-going complement. But carrying a cat on board a ship was already becoming difficult as the laws and regulations that now prohibit such a tradition were beginning to emerge. It was in Australia that they began first to interfere. It became obligatory to declare the carriage of the cat to the authorities at the ship's first Australian port of call. Then, prior to departure from the country, we had to produce documentation to prove the cat was about to sail home with the ship, and everyone seemed happy.

Then, slowly, new regulations emerged. These called for the cat's description to be noted on the documentation and of course we complied, describing Starboard as a ginger male feline. Added to that, it was no longer enough to declare the cat on board prior to departure. Now we had to produce the cat for inspection.

On my last trip on that same ship I nearly fell foul of the new regulations. It was shortly before our final departure from Brisbane that the captain asked me to ensure Starboard was on board and to inform the authorities that he was. I searched the ship for Starboard and even left a conspicuous chunk of cheddar on the floor beside the wardroom door but, much to my growing concern, Starboard was nowhere to be seen. I went ashore and began to call for him in and around the warehouses where I knew he liked to roam in search of prey. Time was running out. Five large buildings later and I was just beginning to despair when I turned a corner and there was Starboard sitting calmly at the foot of a flight of stairs. I snatched him up, ran back to the dock office, got him signed out of Australia and proudly carried him up on board the ship. We sailed homeward-bound within the hour; next stop was the Panama Canal some three weeks distant.

That night Starboard did not come to the wardroom for his cheese and we put it down to the fact that he was probably sulking because his shore leave had been so ignominiously curtailed by me. He did not turn up on the next night or even the next. He seemed happy enough as he patrolled the decks in search of rats and, as usual, allowed the crew to pet and scratch him behind the ears, but he seemed suddenly to have no love for cheese.

It was the captain who first caused me to wonder if I might have captured the wrong cat.

'Have you noticed, lad,' he said, 'Starboard's green eye seems to have turned yellow?' Those fears were cemented when, just as we picked up the pilot to carry us through Panama, I saw our moggie crawl under the canvas covering the life raft on the boat deck. Intrigued to see why, I lifted the corner of the canvas to be met with the sight of our cat snuggled down on her side to allow six ginger kittens to suckle her milk.

A member of the British Guild of Travel Writers, Captain **Michael Howorth** first went to sea in 1968 and later commanded several significantly large, luxury mega yachts owned by the rich and famous. Venturing ashore, he began travel writing and is a specialist in the coverage of superyachts, boutique cruise liners and oceanside resorts.

Jack Sparrow

Rachel A Davis

P^{eep.}

'Is there a bird in here?'

Peep.

We looked at one another, then gazed around the room just like everyone else, feigning curiosity. Yes, there was a bird in the room. There was a four-week-old house sparrow in a cooler bag on my lap, peeping because she was hungry – or perhaps she was also interested in this introduction to the Art Deco architecture of Napier, who can say?

The thing with raising a baby sparrow is that they are always hungry, so they have to go everywhere with you. We were trailing behind a walking tour group, taking in the 1930s architectural details while at the same time feeding a bird in a bag as if it were the most normal thing in the world.

We were two British backpackers visiting New Zealand and staying with friends. Jack the sparrow had fallen from an unseen nest on to the lawn during a storm: a big yellow bill and a tiny, virtually featherless body. With a lot of time on our hands, we took on the task of keeping this little sparrow alive, staying awake through the night feeding it mushed cat biscuits. The days passed and feathers transformed her into a shy but friendly chestnut-brown bird. From the very beginning, we had repeated her name every time we had fed her, in the hope that it would train her, and it had worked. If we called her name, she would flit or hop back to us.

We were preparing to set off in our campervan for a few weeks over the festive period, however. She would have to come with us.

As we drove through the spectacular scenery of the North Island, Jack perched on a wooden spoon between us in the front of the camper, or would hop on to our arms and nap. Sometimes she would snuggle into the nape of my neck and tease my hair with her beak. What a funny sight we looked, the three of us, cruising down the highway!

Arriving at campsites, we would set her down on the grass and she would flit about, testing her wings. When it got dark, Jack would put herself to roost on one particular spot on the curtain wire between the cab and the bed space every night, tucking her head under her wing. If we stayed up late drinking and chatting she would sleepily glare at us with one annoyed eye peeking over her wing. As the sun came up she would start to peep; one of us would sit up and she would hop on to our hand, after which we'd lie back down and the three of us would nap for another hour or so.

On days out, we would pop Jack into the cooler bag and take her along with us, feeding her when she was hungry and letting her out when it was safe to do so. Jack had quite a few adventures with us during those weeks on the road. Early on she joined us on an afternoon tea cruise along the Waikato River on a paddle steamer. This was before she had fledged so there was no worry of her flying into the river. Instead, while I sipped tea and ate scones she perched on my arm and watched the world drift by.

At Waikite Valley Thermal Pools, near Rotorua, Jack took her very first flight to me in the car park. I'd set her down on some grass for a peck about and then called her by name, and she flew up to me – much to the delight of a small party of tourists who had just hopped off a bus. Her sunrise peeping meant that we didn't miss out on an early-morning soak in the blissful geothermal waters – she was the perfect alarm clock.

She also visited Tongariro National Park, under the shadow of Mount Doom, and had a drive around the Coromandel Peninsula where she napped most of the time and missed the beautiful views. Another time, I missed out on visiting Cathedral Cove because it was too warm a day to leave her in the camper and we couldn't leave the windows wide open.

At Waitomo disaster struck. As often happened on campsites, fellow campers would wander over to see the tiny bird perched on either our heads or our shoulders. On this particular occasion Jack had flitted from us on to the head of a woman who had come over to chat. Taken aback, the woman became flustered and, just as Jack hopped off, a gust of wind blew her high into a huge nearby tree. We called her repeatedly, but this was higher than she'd ever flown and we couldn't see her in the dense foliage. We knew that at some point she might fly away, but this was too soon – surely she wasn't ready? We couldn't wait for her, as we were booked on a black-water rafting tour through the subterranean Waitomo Caves, to drift through the darkness under a starry black 'sky' of twinkling glow worms. With very heavy hearts we left Jack in the tree and joined our friends.

Four hours later we returned, after an exhilarating cave experience. I expected her to have vanished, but far across the lawn was a small bird. As I got nearer, I called her name. The little bird lifted its head, then flew towards me and up on to my shoulder.

It was amazing watching her develop as the weeks went on, seeing how instinctively she knew how to preen, how to fly. As she grew, we bought her meal worms and wax moth larvae so she could eat live food, and she loved finishing off our corn on the cob – the inexpensive and abundant bounty of a New Zealand summer road trip.

Having Jack along for the ride made this time in New Zealand really special. She was a perfect travel companion, making so many friends as people loved coming over to meet her.

In the new year we returned to our friends' place, near Cambridge in the centre of the North Island, and spent a month helping them with their smallholding. Jack would join us in the vegetable patch learning to find her own food; any good grubs and bugs we found as we weeded were greedily devoured by our little friend. Pulling into a petrol station in the town one day, the guy at the counter declared, 'You're the people with the bird!'

We couldn't stay in New Zealand forever. I checked, but we couldn't take Jack back to the UK. Our little travel companion had learnt to fend for herself, but she wasn't wild enough to go free. We found her a wonderful home in Taupo, with a woman who rescued birds. Judi updated us via email, sending us pictures. Jack did go wild in the end, but regularly visited the bird feeders in her garden: the one little sparrow who was more fearless than the rest.

Rachel A Davis has lived nomadically for a decade, travelling the world and living a life on the open road in a van. She spends her winters in the far north of Sweden, working for a tour company under the northern lights. Summers are spent wild and free!

From *Tracks*

Robyn Davidson

In 1977, Robyn Davidson trekked seventeen hundred miles across the Australian Outback with four camels and her dog, Diggity. Enduring sweltering heat, fending off poisonous snakes and lecherous men, Davidson's courageous journey of discovery and transformation was driven by a love of Australia's landscape.

I will now, once and for all, destroy some myths concerning [camels]. They are the most intelligent animals I know except for dogs and I would give them an IQ rating roughly equivalent to eight-year-old children. They are affectionate, cheeky, playful, witty, yes witty, self-possessed, patient, hard-working and endlessly interesting and charming. They are also very difficult to train, being of an essentially undomestic turn of mind as well as extremely bright and perceptive. This is why they have such a bad reputation. If handled badly, they can be quite dangerous and definitely recalcitrant... Nor do they smell, except when they regurgitate slimy green cud all over you in a fit of pique or fear. I would also say that they are highly sensitive animals, easily frightened by bad handlers, and easily ruined. They are haughty, ethnocentric, clearly believing that they are god's chosen race. But they are also cowards and their aristocratic demeanour hides delicate hearts. I was hooked.

The incident with the lost camels was slightly more hair-raising than my letters let on. They had been spooked by wild camels in the night and I had slept through the whole thing. The tracks told me what had happened in the morning. I had been letting them go at night either loosely hobbled, or not hobbled at all. My reasoning went this way – we were in a dry desert country and the camels were working hard – they had to range a fair distance from camp to find the feed they needed. And I believed I could now track them over anything.

This business of tracking is a combination of sixth sense, knowledge of the behaviour of camels, keen eyesight and practice. The place we camped that afternoon was gibber country and cement-hard claypan. You could drive a sledgehammer into that stuff and it would hardly leave a dent. Finding the direction they had gone in therefore required circling away from camp until I found the tracks (which had become mixed up with a couple of other cameloid footprints) and trying to follow this general direction, by searching for the scuff marks, looking for freshly eaten fodder and keeping an eye open for fresh dung. (I could tell my camel's dung from any others'.) It required a lot of circular and frustrating walking. As it turned out I found them not too many miles away, stirred up and nervous, heading back to camp. They came straight up to me, like errant children, begging forgiveness. Their friends had left. Rather than putting the fear of god into me, this incident reinforced my confidence in them, and I continued to leave them unhobbled at night. Stupid perhaps, but the camels did gain a little weight that month.

As if walking twenty miles a day wasn't enough, I often went out hunting or just exploring with Diggity after I had unsaddled the camels of an afternoon. On one such afternoon, I had got myself vaguely lost. Not completely lost, just a little bit, enough to make my stomach tilt, rather than turn. I could, of course, backtrack, but this always took time and it was getting dark. In the past, whenever I wanted Diggity to guide me home, I simply said to her, 'Go home, girl,' which she thought was a kind of punishment. She would flatten those crazy ears to her head, roll her amber-brown eyes at me, tuck her tail between her legs and glance over her shoulder, every part of her saying, 'Why are you doing this to me? What did I do wrong?' But that evening, she made a major breakthrough.

She immediately grasped the situation; you could see a light bulb flash above her head. She barked at me, ran forward a few yards, turned back, barked, ran up and licked my hand, and then scampered forward again and so on. I pretended I didn't understand. She was beside herself with worry. She repeated these actions and I began to follow her. She was ecstatic, overjoyed. She had understood something and she was proud of it. When we made it back to camp, I hugged her and made a great fuss of her and I swear that animal laughed. And that look of pride, that unmistakable pleasure in having comprehended something, perceived the reason and necessity for it, made her wild, hysterical with delight. When she was pleased over something or someone, her tail did not go back and forward. It whipped round and round in a complete circle and her body contorted into S-bends like a snake.

I am quite sure Diggity was more than a dog, or rather other than a dog. In fact, I have often thought her father was a vet perhaps. She combined all the best qualities of dog and human and was a great listener. She was by now a black glossy ball of health and muscle. She must have done a hundred miles a day with her constant scampering and bounding after lizards in the spinifex. The trip, of necessity, had brought me much closer to all the animals, but my relationship with Diggity was something special. There are very few humans with whom I could associate the word love as easily as I did with that wonderful little dog. It is very difficult to describe this interdependence without sounding neurotic. But I loved her, doted on her, could have eaten her with my overwhelming affection. And she never, not ever, not once, retracted her devotion no matter how churlish, mean or angry I became. Why dogs chose humans in the first place I will never understand.

© Robyn Davidson (1980) *Tracks* Bloomsbury Publishing Plc.

Robyn Davidson was born on a cattle property in Queensland. She went to Sydney in the late sixties, then returned to study in Brisbane before going to Alice Springs where the events of this book began. Since then she has travelled extensively, has lived in London, New York and India. In the early 1990s she migrated with and wrote about nomads in northwest India. She is now based in Melbourne, but spends several months a year in the Indian Himalayas.